SOARING HIGHER

SOARING HIGHER

Power principles to
rise above adversity

PAT MESITI

EMBASSY BOOKS

SOARING HIGHER
by Pat Mesiti

First Indian Imprint : 2006

This Edition licensed by arrangement with:
Embassy Books LLC,
1626, 38th Avenue North, St. Petersburg,
FL 33713, USA.

Published in India by:
EMBASSY BOOK DISTRIBUTORS
120, Great Western Building,
Maharashtra Chamber of Commerce Lane,
Fort, Mumbai-400 023. (India)
Tel: (022) 32967415/ 22819546
E-mail: embassy@vsnl.com

Cove Art by Deep Image

ISBN 10: 81-88452-71-8
ISBN 13: 978-81-88452-71-2

Printed and bound in India

CONTENTS

MY STORY

Some of you may be acquainted with my books, audio tapes, TV program, charity projects or corporate presentations. For others, this may be the first time you have ever picked up a book authored by Yours Truly. Whichever is the case, let me briefly share a portion of my life with you. You see, I've experienced some of the highest highs and some of the lowest lows. Now I'm not alone in this. Everyone goes through challenging periods in their lives. But I've learned how to bounce back. Even better, I've discovered how to soar above adversity. And I want you to do the same. In fact, I know you can!

Whilst my life has been full of triumphs and tragedies, my experiences aren't unique. For many of us, Ronan Keating's hit song *Life is a Rollercoaster* rings true. Life's like that. We can't ignore that. But wouldn't it be great to be able to bounce back after every challenge? Better still, wouldn't it be great to be able to bounce back higher every time?

2001 was a peak year for me. Everything was going great. I had sold over half a million copies of my four books and I was in the middle of writing my fifth book. I was presenting a national weekly television program. I had sold hundreds of thousands of my own audio tapes and CDs. I was being booked as a corporate speaker a year in advance. I was speaking to audiences totalling over 300,000 a year all over the world: in the USA, the UK, Australia and Asia. I was the director of one of Australia's most successful residential drug and alcohol rehabilitation centres. I had pioneered one of Australia's largest youth organisations in the state of New South Wales in Australia. I had helped build one of the world's greatest churches in Sydney. I was experiencing success in ways that people only dream of.

In October of that year I was in the United States on a speaking tour when a phone call home to Australia changed my life. I had made a mistake – of a personal nature. It began to dawn on me that this was an error that could potentially destroy my career, take away friendships, and – worst of all – break up my family. One day I was standing before a crowd of 80,000 people, the next day I was a revealed as a failure to some of my closest friends and family. Within a week, the media in Australia would be labelling me a failure.

MY STORY

Many began to tell me that my life as I knew it was all over. The frightening thing about it was that no matter what others said - positively or negatively - I could not see any light at the end of my tunnel.

That night in my hotel room I remember thinking, 'I don't want to live anymore!' I didn't want to face another day, mainly because I couldn't see the purpose of another day. I felt the shame of failure suffocate me of any ounce of -self-esteem I once had.

Over the next few days, my world came crashing down around me. A series of resulting phone calls and meetings caused my life to plummet from success mode to frantic mode. It seemed as though everything I tried to do to fix things up actually made things worse. I was in the middle of a nightmare from which I couldn't wake up. The result was that my marriage ended, my business folded, my friendships were tested, and my sources of income dried up. Like a tired boxer battered and bruised, I was out for the count. I hit the canvas hard. Time stood still. It was like I was in a coma.

Then one day I caught a glimmer of hope. You see, as painful as that experience was, there was also a feeling of relief as I began to share my tragedy and bare my soul with a friend. The pressure began to ease. The amazing thing was that the moment I spoke to someone about it, it was like a light began to glow in the darkness, like the sounds of morning stirring through my nightmare. That wonderful experience began a process of healing and restoration.

My friend, I have learned that when your world falls apart, you still have options. One option is to let your life disintegrate and crumble at your feet. The other option is to pick yourself up and start again. I've discovered that it's not what is taken from us that counts, it's what you do with what is left that makes the difference. Sometimes things are taken from us, and sometimes we simply drop the ball. I've dropped the ball and I've dropped the ball big time. Through my own failure I lost it all.

I've come to realise that in the long run it is not the failure itself that counts. What counts is if you get back up. You see, it is much easier to stay down than it is to get back up.

MY STORY

During my crisis, I remember specifically one of my closest friends saying to me, 'Your best days are still ahead of you.' So I got back up.

This book is written to help YOU get back up... to help you experience the exhilaration of success again and again.

INTRODUCTION

I've discovered that most of us don't learn much when life is going well. Unfortunately, most of us learn our lessons the hard way. That's just human nature. We learn more in life through hardship and adversity than we do in times of prosperity and favour. I know I have! Some of my hardships have been self-inflicted, others have been forced on me. But I have learned a lot... because I've made lots of mistakes!

Experts say it takes about 21 days to form a habit. I wonder what it would take to go one step further and completely change life patterns developed over years. I wonder how long it would take to develop a brand new lifestyle, a new way of thinking. More importantly, how do we actually avoid developing habits that will derail a successful life? How do we become successful in spite of our weaknesses and struggles?

The simple answer is: by (finally) learning from our mistakes. This book is about failures and how to overcome them. You see, everybody fails. It's a fact of life. There is no one on this planet who at some point in their journey has not failed. Every famous inventor has failed. Every world leader has failed. Every successful band has failed. But, my friend, a failure is not the person who fails... because then everyone on the planet would be a failure! No, a failure is the person who does not bounce back.

Like you, I have failed. And like me, many of you may be trying to cope with failures of various kinds: relationship breakdowns, bankruptcy, loss of friends or income, failing an academic test, losing a game... Like me, you may be trying to deal with rejection, shame and a broken heart.

But one thing I have discovered is that mistakes are something we do, not something we are. We are all prone to failure. You may ask, 'Why did it happen to *me*?' and 'Why did it have to happen *now*?' One thing I have learned is that answering the why isn't as important as learning to overcome the problem.

What *is* important is how you rebuild your life. And you can best begin to do that by realising the power of lessons learned. The principles I am going to share with you in this book are *life* principles. This book is about the tragedies and mistakes that give rise to triumph, to greatness, to winning.

INTRODUCTION

I want to take you on a journey and share with you the lessons I've learned and am still learning. I'm also going to share with you the experiences of some great men and women in history, and what they learned from their mistakes.

Each chapter is a lesson I have learned. At the end of each chapter I will challenge you to take action, to change your circumstances from failure to success. If you read a chapter every day, you'll find your life will have changed - literally - in 54 days.

LESSON NO. 1

If Humpty Dumpty knew he was an egg,
he would never have climbed the wall

What am I talking about? Simply this: we are all fragile, every one of us. We all encounter challenges and tensions. We all deal with financial pressures and emotional strains. And sometimes we fail.

We have to remember our frailty as human beings and exercise caution in what we expect from ourselves and others. Sometimes we expect our partner or ourselves to be perfect, but we are all 'crackable' under pressure. So it is important to have people and mechanisms in our lives that remind us that we are human, that keep us accountable and help us release tension... otherwise we're headed for a mighty great fall.

Former world boxing champion Mohammed Ali once boarded a plane and was asked by a flight attendant to fasten his seat belt. Ali said, 'Superman don't need no seat belt.' To which the attendant replied, 'Superman don't need no airplane either.' All of us at some point can believe we are Superman or Superwoman. But in fact, like Humpty Dumpty, we are 'crackable'.

What area of your life is starting to show cracks? What reserves are you putting in your tank right now to help you in the long haul? Are you determined that even if you do crack under pressure that you will bounce back better, stronger, smarter?

In his interview with Australian television program, *Australian Story*, Wayne Bennett, the great coach for Australian rugby league club, the Brisbane Broncos, said, 'My life has been adversity. But from each disaster I have come back stronger. I don't fear what is happening, I know how to battle through it. I know my family and I will come out the other side. It is just a matter of when and knowing we will be better for it. We will be stronger people and we will appreciate winning more than we ever have in the past.' That was just after his team had lost seven and drawn one of their first nine games in the 1999 rugby league season.

CHALLENGE

I have learned that it doesn't matter *who* wants you to bounce back, it's whether *you* want to bounce back. It's whether you want to piece your life together again. Everybody's good intentions are irrelevant. The issue is, are you willing to piece your life together again and move on?

Are you determined that Humpty Dumpty will bounce back, and not splatter on the ground? I often wondered why all the kings' horses and all the kings' men couldn't put Humpty together again. It's because they weren't meant to. He was meant to. He was meant to piece his own life together again, and so are you.

LESSON NO. 2

You can't be the best at everything

I've learned that you can't be good at everything. Instead, focus on the one thing that your life can be given to. Find your place in the world and stick to it.

The great American footballer Otto Graham said, 'Everyone can't be the best at everything but everyone can try to be the best at anything. If you give 100% you will get your share of victories.'

If you want your life to be a success, it is important to focus. Often, we spread ourselves too thin. We dilute our potential because we expand ourselves to the point where we lose our strength. So often we run headlong into accepting things at the expense of fulfilling things.

One of the mistakes I made was spreading myself too thin. I began doing too much. I was running six organisations and sitting on the boards of several other worthwhile causes. My intentions were good but I was diluting my strength and my focus to the point where I was no longer fully effective.

Most great people are great at one thing. Mother Teresa didn't feed everybody or run programs for every needy person in Calcutta. She targeted a specific group. If you look at the sporting greats, they are not great sportsmen at everything, they are great at one thing. Pat Rafter, Andre Agassi, Lleyton Hewitt... they are not great football players, but they are fantastic tennis players. They are not good at everything, but they are good at one thing. They don't spread themselves too thin.

You can't be the best at everything. Anyone who thinks he is good at everything generally is an expert at nothing. Have you ever met people who always know what to say in any situation, but whose own lives are not in order? They talk like they are experts in everything, but their lives don't reflect their talk.

A handy man is good at a lot of things, but you would not get him to design, construct and then interior decorate your home. He is good at a lot of things, but he is an expert at none. Make sure you keep your focus.

CHALLENGE

Take a look at *your* life. What can you trim back? What do you need to prune so that you can be fruitful? Are you spreading yourself so thin that you don't have time for family and friends? Do you have time to smell the roses? Perhaps you need to prune some roses. They could be that last project you took on at work, or that extra subject at college. You may even be able to give some of the pruned 'roses' to someone as a gift. Take time now to think about how you can prune your life to make it more rewarding.

LESSON NO. 3

'See everything, overlook a great deal,
and prove a little' - Pope John Paul II

One of the life skills we need is the ability to be observant without being fault-finding. We need to be able to notice things and yet at the same time able to overlook a great deal of what we see. Why? Because some of what we see could be discouraging.

Sometimes you see people getting away with wrongs and misdemeanours. Often you see people doing things you find offensive. You see injustices. Perhaps you see a serious fault in others, but you're blind to that same fault in yourself. Maybe you see someone who becomes successful without really trying, while all your hardest endeavours reap little reward.

If that's you, you may be very observant, but now you need to overlook. You need to overlook situations that can cause you to become disenfranchised or disheartened. Overlook other people's failures, but deal with your own.

Lesson No. 3's quote says 'See everything, overlook a great deal, and prove a little.' So often in life we struggle and strive to prove. I know I did that. Growing up as a child, alcohol ruled our home. This caused me to want to prove to others and to myself that I was better. Perhaps like me you have been on a performance treadmill where you are constantly striving and proving rather than resting in *being*. My friends, you are who you are. You do not have to prove anything to anyone. Instead, rest assured in the security that you are a human being with dignity, value and self-respect. You are a success, not a mistake. You can accomplish great things.

All of us need to understand that greatness is within us. When we are convinced of this truth, we stop trying to prove our greatness to everybody else. We stop comparing ourselves to others and finding fault either in ourselves or them. We begin to overlook rather than criticise.

CHALLENGE

If you want to learn one of the great lessons of life learn to see and enjoy everything, overlook a great deal in others, and stop trying to prove yourself. Just be the person you were created to be.

LESSON NO. 4

Failure is not final, failure is not fatal

Don Shula became the most successful coach in national football history with 325 wins. He said in his book, *Everyone's a Coach*, 'The biggest problem with most leaders of today is they don't stand for anything. Leadership implies movement toward something and convictions provide that direction. If you don't stand for something you will fall for anything.'

Probably his most favourite and pointed statement is, 'Success is not forever, and failure is never final.' Friend, failure is not the end. I know, because I have failed. I have failed in areas of my life that became very public, but that was not the end. I lost my sense of dignity for a while, but that failure was not fatal. I bounced back!

I have discovered that understanding failure is the greatest tool that one can have to resurrect and rebuild. Failure is not fatal and failure is not final. Therefore, failure should never kill your dreams; failure should never kill your goals. Instead, it should be something that causes you to rise up and shout, 'I am not going to die on this mountain!'

During a challenging time in my life, a friend rang me at 2.30 in the morning. He was unaware of the challenges I was facing, but he had had a dream and wanted to share it with me. In the dream, my friend and I were in a fishing boat and I was shot in the head. Now that may sound a bit dramatic, but there was a point to that dream. Over the phone my friend told me, 'Pat, whatever is happening to you right now, I am here to tell you that the wound is not fatal.'

You need to know that your wounds are not fatal either. They are only fatal if you let your wounds kill you. The founder of KFC, Colonel Sanders, failed in his attempt to establish a great franchise, but he did not let it kill him. Inventor of the light bulb, Thomas Edison, failed in many of his experiments. But the great men and women of history never let failure be fatal - instead, they made it a springboard to success.

CHALLENGE

Ask yourself what you can learn from your failures. What amends do you have to make to rectify the problems? What strategies will you implement to ensure this failure does not happen again? Who will you surround yourself with to inspire you to rise above your failure?

Author Alan Redpath once said, 'You will never lighten the load for others until you first feel the pressure in your own soul.' You will never be able to lighten the load of other people's failures until you have failed yourself. It is amazing to me now how most people find me very approachable to talk about their fears, their failures and how to overcome them. As a result of your own failures, try to become that kind of person.

LESSON NO. 5

Don't sell out convictions for conveniences

I've learned that whatever I value I will honour. Learn to place value on your convictions. Isn't it interesting that one kilogram of dirt and one kilogram of diamonds weighs the same, but one of them is of greater value. Decide in your life what is dirt and what is diamonds, and live towards that.

A young Jewish boy grew up in Germany many years ago. He greatly admired and dearly loved his dad, in part because he felt his dad had a great love for religion. Every week the boy's father took his family to the synagogue. During the boy's teenage years the family was forced to move to another area with no synagogue, only a Lutheran church. All the well-to-do people in the new area belonged to it. Suddenly, the boy's father announced that his family was going to become Lutheran because it would be good for business. The young man became very angry, very bewildered and very disillusioned. He later left Germany and went to England to study. Each day he could be found at the British Museum. The young man began to formulate ideas which he eventually developed into a book. He introduced this book with its radical worldviews and a movement was conceived that eventually brought misery to countless millions. His ideas became the norm for governments around the world. This boy's name was Karl Marx.

World history was altered by a father who sold out principles for money, and conviction for convenience. Always understand that the greatest thing you have going for you is your convictions.

Tragically, I once compromised my convictions in an area of my life and I paid a heavy price. It was a tough lesson to learn, but I have learned from that mistake. I have learned to value my convictions. You don't have to make the same mistake. When you try to live for convenience, you pay a price that is often very painful. Make sure that your life is founded on convictions, deeply rooted convictions. Let your business be a conviction, let your financial prosperity be a conviction, let your values be a conviction to you. Don't compromise them. It is better to have them and be wrong in the eyes of many, than to not have them at all. I believe that a man or a woman without convictions will always be unstable and double minded. Make sure you never compromise them, but keep them close to you.

CHALLENGE

Make a list today of some convictions in your life. Here are some of mine:

- I am absolutely convinced that I am uniquely gifted.

- I am absolutely convinced that I should prosper.

- I am absolutely convinced that my business dealings will be successful and prosperous.

- I am absolutely convinced that my children love me, and I am convinced that I love them.

List convictions in your life that are dear to you. Adhere to them and make sure you do not compromise them.

LESSON NO. 6

Always make time for the little guy

People enter our lives every day. Just think of the person that takes your money at the toll booth. If it's a hot summer's day they may be sweating in that booth. Wouldn't it be nice to notice them, smile at them and wish them a great day? One of my dear friends does this all the time. She brings joy to the toll booth attendants because she always has a pleasant smile, a happy tone, and she notices the little guy.

The other week I was at a dinner appointment and I was talking with one of my friends. His son came up to me and said hello. The boy was wearing a bright red jacket and a bright red cap and he looked like he was dressed for success. The sad thing was I shook his hand but I continued speaking to his father. One of my friends challenged me about ignoring the kid and I realised what I'd done was not right. So I went back, made a fuss over his cap and jacket, gave him eye contact, and all night made sure that kid got the attention he needed.

Charles Plumb tells an interesting story. He was a navy pilot in Vietnam. After 75 missions his plane was destroyed and he parachuted into enemy territory. He survived six years in a Communist prison and now he lectures on his experiences. One day a stranger came up to him and said, 'Your name is Plumb. You flew fighter jets from the aircraft carrier *Kittyhawk*, and you got shot down.' Plumb asked how the man knew those things about him. Smiling, the stranger said, 'I packed your parachute, I guess it worked.'

That night Plumb could not sleep. He said he kept wondering what the man had looked like in uniform, and how many times he, as a fighter pilot, had walked past the man, a plain sailor, without speaking. Plumb thought about the hours the man spent in the bows of the ship carrying and weaving the shrouds and folding the silks of each chute—holding in his hands the fate of someone he didn't even know.

CHALLENGE

Friends, make sure that you notice people. Go out of your way to pay attention to people: people who do things for you, people who give you introductions, people who shake your hand, people who greet you. Go out of your way to notice them, and don't make the mistake of not enjoying the experience of others.

So often we look for the famous, the rich and the well-to-do, because we want to hang around them. But always remember that every big shot was once a little shot. Notice people when they are small and seemingly insignificant and they will remember you when they become important, significant and wealthy.

LESSON NO. 7

Brilliance isn't a diploma

Too often we fall into the trap of labelling people. We look at someone's degrees and label them brilliant. We applaud people based on their diplomas, degrees and certificates. But the greatest education is one that life gives us. You can have more degrees than a thermometer, but be as cold as ice when it comes to important things like relationships, love, commitment, understanding... I have come to understand that people don't care how much I know, they care how much I care about them. They care about what is really important, like helping them achieve their goals. They don't want to hear me bragging about my achievements.

Brilliance isn't found in a diploma or an award, it's found in your heart. The word brilliance means 'great brightness; radiance; sparkle'. The word brilliant in French means 'to shine'. Why don't you decide today to go out and shine some light in someone's life.

Think of it folks, Einstein was never brilliant at school and Edison was not much better. Many brilliant people were not considered brilliant academically. There is a story told about a newly hired salesman who sent his first sales report to the home office. It read: 'I seen this outfit which hain't never bot nuthin from us and I sold them a lot of goods. Now I'm goin to Chicawgo.' Before the sales manager could fire him a second letter arrived. 'I cum here to Chicawgo and sole them over a milyon.' Not sure whether to fire the salesman or to retain him, the sales manager dumped the problem in the lap of the company's president.

The following morning the sales department was amazed to see a memo from the president posted on the bulletin board beside the salesman's two letters. It said: 'We ben spendin to much time tryin to spel and not enuf tryin to sel. Lets watch those sails. I want everybody should read these two letters from Gosh who is on the rode doin a grate job for us, and you should go out and do like he dun.'

Brilliance is not about diplomas on walls. It is about get-up-and-go, intuition, initiative, enthusiasm, a 'can do' attitude, and an ability to see things that can be done, without complaining about what can't be done. Don't be concerned about the brilliance you may or may not have as far as an education is concerned. If you have initiative, drive, energy and enthusiasm, if you have a hunger to learn, then you are going to be brilliant. You can't help it if you have all these qualities.

CHALLENGE

Think about the things in your life that are your strengths. Write them down. What are the characteristics of your life that make you brilliant and unique? It is easy to find the negatives, but I want you to make a conscious effort to find the positives and list them.

LESSON NO. 8

When you're through changing, you're through

A story is told of a man travelling on a bus with his three children. The three children were jumping about behaving very unruly. A gentleman looked at them with disdain, thinking to himself, 'Why can't this man control his three children? What is wrong with him?' This man's attitude was controlled by his perspectives. One of his perceptions was that the father obviously didn't discipline his children. So he went to challenge the father, saying, 'Why aren't you dealing with these unruly children?' The father, who appeared to be in a state of shock, looked up at the man and replied, 'I'm sorry that my children are disturbing you and the other people on the bus, but I have just come from the hospital where their mother has passed away and I'm struggling to find a means to tell them.'

The gentleman on the bus had to suddenly change his perception of that father. Like that man, we must all learn to see life through new and different perspectives. Be willing to change your perspective.

All of us need to understand that change is a process. It is not an event, something that happens once, but rather it is a constant process.

The Swedish chemist Alfred Nobel amassed a fortune by inventing dynamite and other explosives used for weapons. When his brother died, a newspaper accidentally printed Alfred's obituary instead. It described him as a man who had become rich by enabling people to kill each other in unprecedented numbers. Deeply shaken, Nobel resolved to dedicate his fortune toward accomplishments that benefited humanity. Hence, the Nobel Prize.

Comedian Jerry Lewis once joked that his best wedding gift was a film of the entire marriage ceremony. He said when things got really bad at home he would go into a room, close the door, run the film backwards and walk out a free man. Now I doubt that any of us will be able to read our obituary in a newspaper or that any of us want to go looking at our marriage ceremony in reverse, but all of us should re-evaluate our lives and make a conscious choice to change things.

As I consider my life, there are things that I have had to change in order to become more effective. I have had to learn to work smarter, not harder. I have

17

had to change from being a driven person to being a leading person. I have had to make changes to schedules and changes to the way I approach life. Being a single dad was not easy and I have certainly changed my opinion on how people cope in single parent families.

CHALLENGE

What is it in your life that needs changing? How are you going to begin that process? Sometimes change is unpleasant, often it is hard, yet almost always it is necessary. Begin the process of change now to become the better person you want to be.

What is it in your business or career that needs to change to make it more profitable? What is it in your attitude that needs to change to make you more effective?

LESSON NO. 9

Size does matter

Accept criticism and disappointment as part of life and when it comes, stand up, look it in the eye, and say, 'You can't defeat me, I am bigger than you.' You see, size does matter. The bigness of your spirit and the size of your heart often determines how you respond when critical words are said about you and people criticise your accomplishments and failures.

Tragically, I heard the story of a young lady who is a brilliant artist, a great painter, but every time she finishes a painting her father criticises it. So now she leaves her paintings unfinished because he can't criticise an incomplete piece of work. Often in our lives we are afraid of criticism, so we start well and then quit. We begin well and then shrink back.

During a period of major transition in my life, I was hounded by the media, criticised and ridiculed publicly, and had a lot of untruths said about me. Everything in me wanted to react with hostility. But I remembered the words of a great friend, a very prosperous and successful businessman. 'Rise tall,' he said.

My friend, rise tall when criticism comes your way. Look it in the eye and say, 'I am bigger than you, I am going to become better because of this.' It's been said that 'the highest reward for a person's toil is not what they get for it but what they become by it'.

When adversity hits, when you drop the ball, know that you are bigger than the situation. Don't make the mistake that many have made, and shrink to the size of other people's opinions, other people's dreams, other people's concepts of what you ought to be and do. Rise tall! Realise that you are bigger than the situation. Understand the power of posture and put yourself above the circumstance, not under it.

CHALLENGE

Think about those situations in your life that you need to rise above. Consider possible responses and estimate what results you will get from them. Surprise your critics by being atypical in your response.

LESSON NO. 10

What you believe at your worst
moment is what you really believe

When our lives are successful and we are doing well, then our beliefs appear as solid as bedrock. But when life derails us and wealth, family and fame are stripped away, often our certainties fade too.

When a winning streak collapses, what do you believe then? Do you still believe the positive things that you once believed? You should, because at your worst moment beliefs are most powerful. In the depths of despair it is the things we believe that really kick in and begin to make a difference. In the midst of my own toughest challenges, what has kept me sane is believing that something good will emerge. And it has! Something good has already emerged and is in the process of becoming something great.

In your worst moments, what do you believe about your life? What do you believe about your faith? What do you believe about yourself? When your marriage begins to fall apart, do you believe that you are still someone of intrinsic value, who can be loved and who has the capacity to love? Do you still believe that you are someone worthy of friendship, even when supposed friends have deserted you? What do you believe when people say negative things about you? Do you believe all the negative stuff or do you believe the positive? What you believe about yourself in your worst moment is what you really believe.

I love the major league baseball player Yogi Berra. He never blames himself when he's not hitting; he just blames the bat. If he keeps missing he changes the bat. Perhaps you think he is not facing reality, but I think Berra has gone one step higher. He knows that he is a champion, but realises that he will not always have winning streaks and he refuses to destroy his own confidence by believing the worst about himself.

CHALLENGE

What do you believe about yourself today? Do you believe the good things? The good things in your life are set, they are great, they are awesome, everybody knows about them. Everything else in life is recoverable. Your losses are recoverable. Your friends are recoverable. Your marriage is recoverable. Finances are recoverable. Don't give in at the worst moment. You will miss the light at the end of the tunnel if you jump off the train half way through.

LESSON NO. 11

All the battles of life are waged within yourself

The great speaker Dwight L. Moody said, 'I have had more trouble with myself than any other man I have ever met.' Sheldon Kopps said, 'All the significant battles are waged within self.' Think about it. Before anything materialises in your life, it generally happens on the inside of you.

Our insecurities come from the inside and often manifest themselves on the outside, perhaps in shyness or aggression, in chatter or pride. I heard someone once say that talent is God-given, so be humble; fame is man-given, be thankful; conceit is self-given, be careful.

Success is a battle fought on the inside of a man or a woman before it ever is an outside battle. What are some of the battles that wage within us? The battle not to quit. The battle not to view yourself as a mistake or a failure. The battle not to navel gaze, not to muse on our circumstances, not to blame others or be full of pride. The battle of loneliness; you and I have to enjoy our own company before we will ever enjoy anybody else's company. The battle for marriage is waged in individual people's lives. A marriage does not break up by accident. It starts in one person breaking down, and then the other breaking down... then you have two broken people breaking down a marriage.

Success in your life is a mindset. You can be successful in the middle of pain. Bill Parcells, one of America's great football coaches, said, 'Don't tell me about the pain, just show me the baby.' He was looking for results.

23

CHALLENGE

What can you do to make sure you win the battles? First, understand that there is a battle. Second, get advice from people who have won battles in their lives. If you're struggling in business and don't know why, go and talk to someone who has some wins and some losses and find out how they came through. Third, don't look for quick fixes to problems, especially long term problems. Be authentic and honest with things in your life. Wear a sign around your neck that says 'Be patient, I am under construction'. Wear it so others can see it, but also realise the same is true for others. Understand that your life is constantly under construction.

LESSON NO. 12

'The weak can never forgive.
Forgiveness is the attitude of the strong.'
– Mahatma Gandhi

It takes strength to forgive others. When people have ripped you off in a business deal, when people have hurt you, it takes strength to forgive them. Do you realise it also takes strength to forgive yourself? Refusing to forgive oneself and move on in life is an act of cowardice. Sure, you can never forget things. You are not a computer that can erase its memory bank, but you must forgive.

You see, forgiveness is a bridge that every single one of us has to cross. You can expend your energy blaming others for things that go wrong in your life, for your lack of success, or financial woes. Or you can choose to forgive others when they have wronged you. Forgiveness is your choice.

Some scientists set out to capture a rare species of monkey and bring it back alive and unharmed. To do this they devised a trap, a little jar with a narrow neck into which they placed a handful of nuts. The monkeys would smell the nuts and reach in to get them, but they could not withdraw their clenched fists. They were trapped, unable to escape and unwilling to let go. Sometimes human beings are just like those monkeys. We are unable to escape our past mistakes, fears and failures because we are unwilling to let go.

Have you been mistreated and vowed never to *forget* the abuse as long as you live? Whether you know it or not, you are harbouring unforgiveness and that is a sign of weakness. Don't be a carrier of that disease.

CHALLENGE

Here are some tips on how to forgive:

- Realise you have a file called Dirty Rotten Things People Have Done To Me. Burn the file by choosing to forgive.

- Understand that forgiveness is something you will need from others and others will need from you for the rest of your life, so learn to be good at it.

- Understand that the person who says 'I will forgive but never forget' is actually telling the truth. But they should emphasise, 'I will forgive, and I will choose to forget - to forget the pain, forget the anger and move on.'

LESSON NO. 13

Your destiny is seldom linked to
those who walk away from you

Have you ever had business partners or close friends who one day walked away from you? Let me help you get over the pain of that by telling you your destiny is no longer linked to those people. Certain people will leave you, and when they do, let them go. Don't try and talk them into staying, because you may end up trying to do that for the rest of your life.

Your destiny is seldom tied to those who walk away from you. When people don't belong in your life anymore, not even a truckload of super glue is going to make them stay. There will always be people who share our lives and then move on. That part of the story comes to a close, but the story and the journey continues. Never beg people to stay against their will. Sometimes the gift of goodbye opens up another door. Move on, but don't move away.

Here is what I suggest you do. Accept partings as part of life. Get up, go out, have a great meal, treat yourself to a night out with some good friends, and start living again. There is something better in store for you.

If, however, you know that your destiny and dreams are linked to a person, then be with them, hang with them. You won't have to beg them to stay, they will want to stay. You won't have to pull strings behind the scenes to get them to stay. They will willingly accept you and look for your friendship. Hang around those kinds of people and realise they are the ones who will help you to get active and living again.

Within some relationships there are times of divorce, and divorce is like an amputation. You survive, but there is less of you, and it actually feels worse if you didn't want the divorce.

CHALLENGE

If someone close has abandoned you, you have to understand that life goes on, that dreams live on. And you have to forgive. You see, you have to acknowledge your mistakes, and take time to rebuild. Start living and giving again. That's the best way in which to build a great destiny and a great future.

LESSON NO. 14

Discipline launches you, it doesn't restrict you

Bob Knight, the legendary and often crazy US college basketball coach, states that the most important single ingredient in athletics is *discipline*, but he adds, 'I have many times felt that this word is the most ill-defined in all our language.' To me, *discipline* means doing what has to be done, when it has to be done, as well as it can be done, and doing it that way all the time. Discipline is a no nonsense attitude with tunnel vision. It is focused.

When allied troops captured a young American fighting alongside the Taliban, a major American newspaper wrote, 'They didn't put their foot down when he announced he was going to drop out of school. They didn't interfere when he decided he was going to become a Muslim. They were actually proud of him for pursuing an alternative course. His mother said it was good for a child to find a passion. They didn't object when he asked them to pay his way to Yemen nor when his new circle of friends included gunmen. As long as he could remember his oh so progressive parents had answered 'yes' to his every whim, every fancy and every passion. The only thing they insisted on was that nothing be insisted on.'

Newsweek called it truly perplexing that the young man was attracted to a narrow intolerant sect. In actual fact, there is nothing perplexing or confusing about it. That young man craved standards and discipline. His Mum and Dad had been unable to give him any, but the Taliban did. His road to ruin did not begin in Afghanistan; it began when his parents never said no.

The road to ruin begins when we don't learn to say no - no to wrong passions, no to wrong thinking, no to bad spending. All of these things have consequences. Someone once said that sooner or later in life we all sit down to a banquet of consequences. Make sure the consequences you face are positive, and the key to that is to discipline yourself.

I have learned to be up at 5 o'clock every morning regardless of how late I get to sleep the night before. I am disciplined with what I eat, because I want my body to last a long time.

I have become more disciplined with money and more disciplined in relationships. Because of past immoral failure I am now more disciplined with my eyes and my ego. I am more controlled in what I say and, more importantly, what I don't say. Discipline, my friends, will never hinder you, it will always launch you.

CHALLENGE

List those areas in your life that require more discipline. It may be your diet, your fitness, money management, relationships, sleep patterns, reading, writing, face-to-face communication... Be honest, because increased discipline in those weak areas will most certainly lead you to more successes than you have experienced before.

LESSON NO. 15

There is nothing that has ever happened
to you or to anyone else that cannot be forgiven

In his brilliant book *Even Eagles Need a Push*, businessman and author, David McNally, tells a wonderful story about LeLy Hayslip. LeLy Hayslip speaks on forgiveness as easily as she speaks on personal tragedy. During the Vietnam War, soldiers tortured her by sending electric shocks through wires attached to her body. She was then tied to a stake in the hot afternoon sun and honey was poured on her feet to attract biting ants.

Lely has had more than 20 years to heal the physical and psychological wounds caused by these and other gross indignities, and has put her experiences into a book titled *When Heaven and Earth Changed Places*. The power of forgiveness in her life has been such that it inspired a vision to build a bridge between Vietnam and the United States to heal the Veterans and the Vietnamese people. In her words, 'We must forgive every single human being in the whole world, not just in Vietnam and the United States, but the whole planet; we are here together.'

In spite of the indignities that Nelson Mandela suffered, he shows no hint of bitterness towards his jailers, calling instead for a life of dignity and understanding with all people. Your heart's memory must eliminate bad things, magnify the good, and must always be thankful that in spite of what others do to you or what you may have done to others there is still hope in the future. Forgiveness is a thing that cleans the deck of our lives. Resentment and anger always hurts *us* more than the other person we refuse to forgive.

Dr Bernie Siegel, in his incredible work with cancer patients, says, 'You can learn to forgive yourself. You can't change your shortcomings until you accept yourself despite them.' Learning to forgive yourself, learning to forgive others, helps us soar into a positive future, a life of greater fulfilment. There is nothing more bitter than a bitter person.

I remember during one of my periods of restoration and rebuilding how one of my friends challenged me about how bitter I was becoming. I immediately defended myself, but in my reply I heard exactly what she had heard and realised what I was becoming.

I had to uproot bitterness from my life or it would have become a tree that would bear ugly fruit, not just in my life, but in my children's lives, my business life, in my speaking life. I refuse to get bitter and I choose to forgive.

CHALLENGE

Take an honest look at your own life. Are you becoming bitter over a past failure? Because if you are, it will hold you back from achieving real success. Worse still, it will affect your relationship with those around you. Deal with it, forgive those who have hurt you, and move on and upward.

LESSON NO. 16

Money magnifies what you are already

Australian rugby league coach Wayne Bennett says that a man's treatment of money is the most desirable test of his character. How we make money and how we spend it says a great deal about who we are. Money is not the problem in life. It's what we do with it. Money is a good thing. Over the past few years a lot of money has come through my hands and I have chosen to not be a pool, but a stream through which money can flow to others.

When people say there is too much money in sport, I have to laugh. Money is not the problem in sport. Money does not corrupt athletes. Great men and women of character will always be great men and women of character. If someone already has a seed of corruption in his or her heart, whether they are athletes, ministers or business people, then money will often be used in the wrong way. Money magnifies what you are already, no more and no less. A generous man will be generous with a little and generous with a lot. A tight person will be tight with a little and tight with a lot.

There are two ways to get more money: one is to accumulate more, and the other is to desire less. To be wiser in your spending, be more attentive about where the money flows to, not just where it flows *from*. Here are some secrets to creating wealth:

- Work
- Give
- Budget
- Don't spend more that you make
- Invest wisely
- Don't fear losing money
- Be generous of heart, generous of mind, and generous with money.

Give strategically. Give where you know there will be reward and give where you will get a sense of fulfilment. There is nothing wrong or corrupt about money. Always remember money magnifies what you are.

Today, think about where you can make more money, where you can budget better, where you can be a little bit more generous. My golden rule in life is this: If you are generous to others, they will always be generous to you.

CHALLENGE

Decide where you will give next – in the short-term and in the long-term. Then determine how much you will give, as well as what you will give: money, time, resources, skills... And decide all this by imagining what will give you the most satisfaction. The satisfaction of giving generously is a joy only a few ever experience... become one of those few!

LESSON NO. 17

**No matter how much you have learned from the past,
it will never tell you all you need to know for the present**

Author Leroy Eims said, 'A leader is one who sees more than others see, who sees further than others see, and he sees before others do.' All of us have experiences in our lives that we have learned from. You and I, as we grow as people, as leaders and business people, must see more, see further than others, and see before others. But for many of us there are times in life when we really don't know what to do when things happen to us. I heard a friend deliver a funny message he titled 'What to do when you don't know what to do'. So what exactly do we do during those times in our lives when we don't know what to do?

Author John Maxwell says that we have to learn to navigate, to take life one step at a time. Jack Welch, former Chairman and CEO of General Electric, said that 'a good leader remains focused'. Controlling your direction is better than being controlled by it. For many of you, something has just happened to you and you are not sure how to deal with it. Determine that you are going to control the direction, that you are going to go forward. Someone once said, 'I don't care which way we go in life as long as we go forward'. Don't allow present circumstances to hinder progress in your life.

Remember to live life one day at a time. Don't lock your focus only on a long-term view. Enjoy each moment, including the moment you've got right now. I've come to learn that I was so focused on the future that I forgot to enjoy my present: time with my kids, time with myself, time to do nothing but enjoy the moment. In my frantic pace, travelling 150,000 miles a year on one airline alone, running organisations, turning organisations from bankruptcy into profit, I forgot to smell the roses and enjoy the present, to sit down and sip a coffee slowly rather than gulp it down in a hurry.

I've always enjoyed the company of my close friends and my children. But when it seemed I could have lost them all, I quickly realised how important those relationships were and how much I valued them. Someone once said that we never know what we've got until it's gone. I pray that will not be the case with us any more, but that we learn to enjoy our present and learn to enjoy what we have.

35

CHALLENGE

One of the things you can learn from your past is to enjoy your present. Be prepared to take time out to think through your present circumstances. Be pro-active in your progress rather than reactive. Think through the processes and answers and results in a systematic way. Take time to talk to people about aspects of your life. Enjoy the company of those who actually matter to you.

LESSON NO. 18

The most common responses to life crises
are denial, Resistance and Acceptance

Each one of us faces crises in life that take different forms and different shapes. For an adult, crises could be facing bankruptcy, loss of a friend, or a death in the family. For a man, a crisis could be the loss of a job. To a teenager, a crisis might be to have a pimple on a first date. In a way perplexing to men, some ladies face a crisis when they break a nail on an important outing or cannot find the right pair of shoes to match a dress. In these latter examples, time often reveals a latent humour in the crisis that we never realised when struggling to overcome it.

There are three common responses to crises. The first is denial. We tend to bury our heads in the sand and hope the problem will somehow mysteriously and painlessly disappear in a short period of time. The second common response is resistance. This is when we fight what's happening or fight ourselves in a futile effort to somehow regain something that is lost. The third response is acceptance. We may not necessarily like our situation, but we acknowledge it is real and we are willing to deal with the truth of what is going on around us no matter how severe or how difficult that problem might be.

Amazingly, denial and resistance generally prolong the pain and delay the resolution of a crisis. In contrast, acceptance of these crises opens the door for us to hope. Harrison E Salisbury said, 'There is no short cut to life. To the end of our days, life is a lesson imperfectly learned.' How true are his words - we have to move out of denial and resistance and learn to accept and move on. For me, life is a continual process of change. I've learned to be brutally honest, to accept not just my failures and shortcomings, but also my strengths.

I have been wiped out financially, emotionally and even spiritually, but each time I have looked back on what made me successful, regathered those principles that made me successful, and put them into operation again. I have had to hang on to what I believe. During one of my worst crises, I spent a lot of time in the unwilling and unresolved attitude of resistance. At times I blamed others for my situation, but mostly I blamed myself. Yet blame is ineffectual; it's a form of resistance because it doesn't really change anything.

At times I lingered in denial refusing to believe what was happening. I hoped it was a bad dream that would go away. It wasn't until acceptance hit me that I could begin to rebuild, realign and reassess.

It has been said that the pace at which we learn is in direct proportion to our determination to rise above doubt and transcend the limitations. Part of learning is to become responsible for our own lives and actions. Whether you like it or not, you are ultimately responsible for your actions and decisions, regardless of circumstances.

The great poet John Keats said, 'Failure... is, in a sense, the highway to success, inasmuch as every discovery of what is false leads us to seek earnestly after what is true'. When you live in denial and resistance you delay finding out what is actually true.

CHALLENGE

Don't live in denial, don't keep resisting: learn to accept and move on. Make sure you are the kind of person who moves on to acceptance and therefore on to change.

LESSON NO. 19

If I have to move more than two feet away from where I am to be happy, I'm never going to be happy

Author Kin Hubbard said, 'It is pretty hard to find what does bring happiness; poverty and wealth have both failed.' If you ask anyone in life what their real goal is they will generally say 'to be happy'. We men struggle to find happiness in our search for a beauty to win or a princess to rescue. Maybe women try to find happiness in the right kind of partner or in a career. Some people think they can find happiness in money. I can assure you that money doesn't necessarily bring you happiness but, then again, neither does poverty. So this is not to downplay money. I believe that money can make you a lot happier than poverty. But we all have to understand that happiness doesn't come from external factors or from any other person: it comes from ourselves. If you have to look to another person to be happy, you are never going to be completely happy. If you are going to have to find a career to be happy, you are never going to be happy, because happiness should be an outflow of what you already are. It was Doris Mortman who said, 'Until you make peace with who you are, you will never be content with what you have.'

Success can bring you a form of happiness, but the reality of happiness must already be latent within you. My dictionary defines success as 'a favourable result, a wished for ending'. Most people associate happiness with the ultimate wished-for ending in life - the fairytale cliché 'and they lived happily ever after'. But I believe happiness is the result of daily choices and decisions. To others it may mean achieving a certain goal. But understand that true happiness come from inside you; it is not based on externals. Happiness is not necessarily going to be based on what you have and what you don't have. You can be poor and happy, or poor and miserable. You can be rich and happy, or rich and miserable. Understand that happiness is about what we are and what we desire to become, and finding fulfilment in that.

Show me a man or woman without passion, without business, without a sense of accomplishment, and I will show you a miserable person. But you show me someone with a passion for life, with a cause, who is actively pursuing that cause, and I will show you a happy person. Remember, if you have to move more than two feet from where you are to be happy, then you will never be happy.

CHALLENGE

Decide today if you are willing to change on the inside in order to experience happiness. Decide today to accept that happiness is up to you alone.

LESSON NO. 20

The future awaits the burial of my past

Inventor of the spark plug and automatic transmission, CF Kettering, stated, 'My interest is in the future because I am going to spend the rest of my life there.' Think of that, your interest has got to be in the future because that is where you are going to spend the rest of your life. The great Winston Churchill had to learn this. Most people are unaware that Churchill faced incredible obstacles in his personal life. We only view him in light of his leadership and public success in World War II. We see the snap shot of the hero during that time of great trial, but we need to see the movie length version of his life.

Churchill was a man of steely will who led his nation to triumph against Hitler. But years before that victorious moment, he plunged through a succession of pitfalls, each one worse than the last. In August 1929, Churchill managed to acquire approximately $70,000. It was an unimaginable figure for one single month's work. He invested nearly all of the money in American stock and wrote a note to his wife saying how pleased he was to have reached a place of financial independence. Ninety days later the stock market fell and Churchill lost virtually everything. He experienced ninety days of financial security, then the bottom fell out. That alone could cause someone to spiral into the depths of despair, but two more devastating blows were to follow.

In 1931, after serving his entire adult life as a central figure in the British Government, Churchill was denied a Cabinet post. He was banished to the political wilderness while Adolf Hitler was building his war machine. Churchill, the only British politician who saw the reality of such a tyrant, was put out to pasture. Then that same year, while trying to hold things together financially and while fending off depression from his political defeat, Churchill took a tour of Canada and the United States.

In New York City he looked the wrong way before crossing the street and was hit by a taxi travelling at 35 miles an hour. He landed in hospital where he clung to his life by a thread. Churchill was 57 years old, and in three years three life-shattering experiences had devastated him. Yet he recovered from those episodes. Nine years later, at the right moment in history, the government that had ignored him turned to him in desperation to save not only the future of England but that of the Western World. But that never would have happened if Churchill had not buried the past.

CHALLENGE

Perhaps you have experienced some devastating setbacks, some death blows. Don't bury your dreams, don't bury your hopes, and don't bury aspirations. Instead, bury your past. Your future depends on it.

LESSON NO. 21

The door of opportunity hangs on small hinges

We live in a world where we always look for the big break, the big show, and the big crowds. Now let me say that bigness isn't wrong, bigness is great. But the amazing thing about life is that big things generally start from small things. Never despise the day of a small beginning. Your life was created from a very small cell. It's amazing to think that an atom can destroy a whole nation, that a large acorn tree grows from a very small seed.

The door to great opportunities actually rests on small hinges. What is now the huge empire known as Coca-Cola started very small. What is now known as the Microsoft Corporation started as a very small idea in a young guy's head. Think of that, the bigness of a corporation with annual profits that dwarf the budget of many nations came from the smallness of an idea.

What ideas come to us, what opportunities arrive at our doorsteps that we bypass because they are too small? The opportunity may be to give someone a smile, to lend a helping hand, to do a good deed for someone in need. These are small opportunities that we must never despise nor discard. Look for the opportunities that arrive on a very small hinge, because they could open up a tremendous door for you. Discard the small things and you really discard the great things of life.

Many people want to start at the top. One of my good friends said to me once, 'The only position in life where you start at the top is grave digging.' All of us have to start at the bottom with small things and work our way up. Life doesn't owe us anything, we owe life everything. Make the most of the smallest opportunity so you can turn it into the greatest of successes.

The average couple spends about 37 minutes a week in meaningful communication. They spend five times longer each day watching television. Wouldn't it be wonderful to take those moments in front of the TV and turn them into meaningful conversation with our families or to sow those moments into a business venture!

CHALLENGE

Take the opportunity today to talk to your spouse and kids; make the most of your time with them. Engrave into your psyche that the door of opportunity hangs on the smallest of hinges, and that door can open to huge avenues of success. Determine to look for small opportunities each day... and to make the most of them.

LESSON NO. 22

Educators teach with chalk and books,
life teaches through adversity and challenges

I never really liked school. When I was a child, I spent more time away from school than I did in school. And I know many other students were the same. If we are honest with ourselves, many of us did not enjoy listening to the teacher, having them chalk lessons on a board, or give us homework when we wanted to go out and play. Most of us will admit that we've forgotten a lot of the things we learned at school.

But if you look back over your life you'll discover that you learned many important things through adversity and challenge. Benjamin Franklin once said, 'Those things that hurt instruct.' And boy, was he right! For example, marriages start because of love, but continue because of commitment. Businesses start because of opportunity, but they continue to succeed because of drive, vision and the birth of new ideas and concepts. Each one of those things has its own challenges.

CHALLENGE

Here is what I suggest we do when life presents us with challenges, especially in the area of relationships.

First, attack the problem, not the people. Remember, we are all on the same team. Don't take your frustration out on people. Second, make sure you get all the information you need. I often speak to business consultants who tell me that before you determine solutions you must have all the facts. This applies to life, to business, and to relationships. Get all the facts and think before you speak. Nothing is more dangerous than second-guessing or jumping to conclusions. Third, list all your options. When you list your options you will probably be less emotional and more objective. Be clear in your own mind about the outcome you want.

Fourth, remember to look for the positive in all situations. When you are facing challenges in life - whether personal or business - it is easy to only see the negatives. But M. Scott Peck says, 'It is only because of problems that we grow mentally and spiritually'. It is through the pain of confronting and resolving challenges that we learn.

No matter how bad things are, my friends, or how bad things may seem at the time, every situation holds a positive, so look for it. Every photograph that you have is a negative in reverse. Learn to see life in reverse when you are looking at a negative.

Lastly, once you've recognised the positives, never hold back from doing good. In spite of the challenge you face, whether in business, marriage or other relationships, don't hold back from doing good because you will be sowing a seed for the future.

LESSON NO. 23

You don't need to preface honesty

Someone once said, 'Always tell the truth and you won't need a good memory'. In my past, because of some character failures I have since dealt with, I sometimes felt I had to cover myself by not telling the whole truth. Unfortunately, that can become a negative pattern. Probably like me, you may also have been in situations in which you felt you had to try to cover yourself. Now, we are not necessarily lying, but we are not necessarily telling the truth either.

In the movie *A Few Good Men*, Tom Cruise challenges Jack Nicholson about the truth, and Jack Nicholson demands, "What do you want?" Tom Cruise replies, "I want the truth!" Jack Nicholson, in that incredible piece of cinematography, declares, "You want the truth? You can't handle the truth!"

Most of us are familiar with the quote from Shakespeare's Hamlet: 'To thine own self be true.' I have learned that a lack of honesty will always, like a boomerang, come back. If you want to sink a boat, all you need is a small pinhole at the bottom of the boat. What starts as a pinhole, ends up as a disaster.

Don't allow your conscience to be numbed by a lack of integrity. A friend of mine who is a public speaker once boarded a bus and gave the driver $2 for a $1 ticket, expecting to receive $1 in change. However, the bus driver gave him change of $3. My friend sat at the back of the bus and thought, 'Wow, what a blessing.' But he realized that he had better be honest with the bus driver, so he approached the bus driver and said, 'Mr driver, I gave you $2, the bus ticket is $1, and yet you gave me $3 back in change. So you gave me more money than I originally gave you'. The driver replied, 'I know I did.' 'You do?' my friend asked, surprised. 'Yes, I heard you speak last night on honesty'.

Have you ever heard people say, 'To be perfectly honest with you...'? The truth is, you are either honest or you are not. You can't be imperfectly honest. You are either telling the truth or you are not. Truth needs no preface; it needs no introduction. It speaks for itself.

Honesty is not the best policy, it is the only policy. I have learned in life that once you open the door to dishonesty about your feelings, your needs and your struggles, you are not only lying to others, you are also lying to yourself. Remember, be honest to yourself and you will always be honest to others. Honest people stand out in a crowd... and they attract. If you are looking for a life partner, who would you rather choose: a dishonest person or an honest person? If you are choosing a business partner, who would you choose?

CHALLENGE

Can I encourage you to be honest in your business dealings and to be honest in your relationships. Then go to a higher level and be honest to yourself. The big lesson is this: 'What you don't learn through truth, you will experience through pain.' Choose truth!

LESSON NO. 24

Handicaps only disable us if we let them

Not long ago I was speaking to some friends of mine who are very successful network marketers. I was sharing with them about some challenges I had just experienced. I related to them how in the midst of success my whole life seemed to fall apart. 'I don't want to live in the past and dwell on my mistakes,' I told them. My friends, Helen and Peter, looked at me and it was as if they could see into my heart. Helen said, 'Your past will only hinder you if you let it.'

Roger Crawford is a successful author who speaks to Fortune 500 companies. A professional tennis player, he travels the world as a consultant. That may not impress you, but what if you knew he had no hands and only one foot? When Roger Crawford was born his doctor told his parents that he would never be able to walk or take care of himself, but they disagreed. Crawford's parents sent him to regular schools and involved him in sport and taught him to think positively. They never allowed him to feel sorry for himself or take advantage of his handicap.

One day Crawford received a call from a man who had an identical handicap. Crawford got excited thinking perhaps he had found someone older who might act as his mentor. But when the two met, Crawford discovered he was wrong. 'I found someone bitter, who blamed all his disappointments on his body,' said Crawford. 'He couldn't hold a job and he blamed that on discrimination and not, as he admitted, because he was constantly late, absent and failing to take responsibility. His attitude was 'the world owes me!' His problem was that the world disagreed.' The man was actually angry with Crawford because he didn't share in his despair.

Friends, this man became a prisoner to his attitude rather that a prisoner to his circumstances. Our handicaps, our disappointments, our challenges can only disable us if we let them. The real limitations are in our minds and in our hearts.

CHALLENGE

I want you to think about what has limited you. What excuses have you come up with? What reasons do you have for not getting out of the rut you're in? The only handicap you have is in your heart. You need to disable that handicap and realise that the ability given to you is unique. You alone can seize the opportunities that life has for you.

LESSON NO. 25

What moment will define your life?

A little while ago while driving in my car, I switched on the radio and was shocked to hear a national radio broadcaster slamming me with all kinds of accusations, misinformation and lies. I was reluctant to call the radio station to correct the error because I thought it would simply aggravate the situation. All of a sudden something rose up within me. In a torrent of aggression, vision and drive, I yelled out at the top of my voice, 'My failure will not define my life!'

Failures have never defined any great person's life. The failures of Babe Ruth did not define his life, his home runs did. The failures of Albert Einstein, Winston Churchill, and Thomas Edison did not define their lives, their successes did. Everyone in life fails. We all miss the mark sometime. But we don't define life by the misses; we define life by the bulls-eyes, by the targets we hit, the slam dunks, the home runs, and the holes putted.

There is a story told of two men, Dan Rhodes and Dave Thomas, who met long before Thomas opened up his first Wendys shop. Rhodes admitted he always knew that young Thomas would some day be something big, but he passed up the opportunity to invest in Wendys. Later Rhodes met Colonel Sanders and had a chance to buy his stock before it went public. Rhodes turned down that opportunity too because he didn't agree with some of the Colonel's ideas. When he was in the restaurant business, Rhodes met a salesman named Ray Crock. Rhodes admits that Crock was a nice guy, but he chose not to invest in his little hamburger joint called McDonalds. A few years later, on an Alaskan cruise, Rhodes met an attorney from Seattle who suggested Rhodes invest in his son's new computer company. It was called Microsoft; again Rhodes declined the offer.

Right now, most of us would be thinking that Rhodes was a fool. But he learned from his mistakes and kept pursuing his dreams. Eventually, Rhodes saw his name on *Forbes Magazine's* list of the 400 most successful business owners in America. He didn't let his failures define his life.

CHALLENGE

Friend, this is a question I want to ask *you*. What moment will define *your* life? Will it be your failures at school, your broken relationship, a bankruptcy, a missed opportunity, the loss of a loved one, or an abusive situation? You must not let moments of negativity define your life. You must make those moments your building blocks for a great purpose.

Start seeing your failure as an investment in the future. You will most certainly get another chance to build again, only this time make it better than the last time.

LESSON NO. 26

Your future is connected to *some* people, not *all* people

Isn't it amazing that when you help others achieve their goals, more than likely you end up closer to your own goals. There is a connection here... people helping each other. It's called 'networking'. I have often heard people say, 'It's not *what* you know, it's *who* you know.' It's a sad fact that people with brilliant gifts don't always get to fully realise their potential if their talent remains hidden and undiscovered. There are people with incredible singing voices, sometimes more gifted than many of our current pop stars, and yet they never achieve their goals. Why? Often it's because they weren't connected with others who could have helped them realise their dreams. It's about connections. Understand that if you want to expand your life, you have got to stay connected.

Life is a bit like a plant. It needs to be connected to the soil for it to be fruitful. It can only grow if it remains connected to the soil because soil provides it with stability, water and nutrients. As you read this book, you may be in a situation in which you need waters of refreshing, new relationships. Well, stay connected. You may need some sunlight, new revelation, insight and inspiration on products, services, staff, relationships... stay connected. You may feel you are surrounded by fertilizer right now. Your life may stink. Just remember, you need to stay connected, to sit through the natural processes of life - including discomfort. Stay connected with the right kind of people in the right environment - the right soil – and once the smell and discomfort has gone, you won't remember the stench of the fertilizer. Instead you will savour the sweet smell of success... if you stay connected.

Andrew Carnegie said that it marks a big step in your development when you realise that other people can help you do a better job than you can do by yourself. After all, you can't whistle a symphony, it takes an orchestra.

All of our futures are interconnected, but not to everybody. Our futures are connected to the people that matter in life. A story is told of Billy Graham, one of the most respected and honourable figures in modern history, who one day asked his childhood friend Grady Wilson to join his team. At first Wilson refused because he had a successful organisation himself. But Graham persisted and eventually Wilson made a decision to follow Billy Graham. He set aside his dreams in order to be part of another man's dream. That decision made a huge difference not only in his life but also in the lives of millions of others.

Sometimes in our life we have to pursue a smaller dream in order to fulfil a bigger one. Generally, that dream is tied to one special person or a number of special people.

I was very privileged to work alongside a few gifted people who helped me grow the organisations I headed up. I am increasingly thankful that our worlds connected because they helped me build organisations that impacted the lives of thousands through my books, tapes and presentations. My future depends on connecting with a few more people like that.

CHALLENGE

If you want to build a great life, learn to give yourself to others, to serve others, to honour others. Understand that those people with whom you truly connect will be few, but these few connections will cause a ripple effect. Like a pebble thrown in a pond, your future will affect some people, and through them many others.

LESSON NO. 27

You can't steer a parked car

During one of the moments of crisis in my life, the feeling of despair and failure rendered me very immobile. I became a dejected person and this frustrated me. On top of that, I struggled with depression, to the point where I couldn't get through the day without anti-depressants. It's easier now to look back and tell you what was happening to me: I was focussing on my current situation, on my pain. My mind became immobile. It wasn't moving forward, it wasn't creating, and that only caused me to fall into even further discouragement and deeper depression. I wondered how I was ever going to get out of that situation.

But here's what I did: I decided I had to stop looking at the current problem and start looking forward. I had to create a dominant image in my mind that was going to propel me forward. The next thing I did was to develop an action plan. The third thing I did was to surround myself with the kind of people who were going forward, and who weren't going to just feel sorry for me. I can tell you, friend, it worked!

What would your children think of you if you went into the garage and began to steer the car? You don't turn the ignition on, you aren't moving, but night after night you get into that car and move that wheel to the left and to the right. Surely your wife, your children and your friends would think you are crazy. You're not going forward just sitting and steering!

So many people do that in life. They want to get ahead, they want to be successful, they want to make a lot of money, they want to be known for great things, they want to achieve... but they forget to turn the ignition on in order to get moving. So many people have the attitude of 'one day I'm gonna... one day I will'.

If you want to get ahead you have to get moving. You can't steer a parked car. You can't give the vehicle of your life direction unless you get it moving forward. It's no good spinning your wheels. Too many people just spin the wheels. They burn a lot of rubber, make a lot of noise and blow a lot of smoke, but they're not going forward.

CHALLENGE

It's time to get your dream on the road again. Don't keep it parked in the garage of disappointment, despair, frustration and let-down. Turn the ignition on, put the pedal to the metal, get moving and steer yourself towards a great destiny.

LESSON NO. 28

It's too soon to quit

A few years ago, a rap artist brought out a song called 'I'm too ligit to quit'. It's a catchy phrase and worth pondering if you're thinking of throwing in the towel. An unknown poet wrote:

> Many a failure turns about,
> When he might have won if he'd stuck it out
> So stick to your task,
> Though the pace seems slow,
> For you may succeed with one more blow.

That's the story of Irwin Rosenberg, a junior officer discharged from the American navy when he was diagnosed with cancer. Rosenberg was determined to get back his health and get back to his job. At one point, he was given two weeks to live but with sheer determination and faith his cancer was bought under control. Restored to health, Rosenberg focused his attention on becoming a naval officer again, but he discovered that regulations forbid the re-instatement of a person discharged with cancer. Someone told Rosenberg to give up, as it would take an Act of Congress to get him re-instated. But that advice gave Rosenberg a new target. He pursued an Act of Congress. After years of waiting, petitioning, cutting through red tape and battling the ever-present bureaucracy, President Truman signed into law a special Bill that allowed Irwin Rosenberg to re-enlist in the navy. The man went on to become a Rear Admiral in the United States Seventh Fleet.

The poem I began this lesson with goes on to say:

> You can never tell how close you are,
> It may be near when it seems afar
> So stick to the fight and when you are hardest hit,
> It's when things seem worst that you mustn't quit.

Sometimes we are so close to a breakthrough, almost paper-thin close to a breakthrough, and we quit. Imagine if the great tenor Pavarotti quit on his first singing lesson or Wayne Gretski gave up on his first attempt at ice hockey. What if Michael Jordan had quit in high school because he couldn't make the grade? All of us would have been robbed of the joy their achievements and brilliance have bought us.

CHALLENGE

You must not quit either. Don't quit on your dreams, on life, on your business, on hope... because it not only robs you, but others too. Your future is connected to others. It is important that you daily have a resolve that says, 'I'm too ligit to quit'. You see, you are not a failure because you fail; you are a failure if you give up. So, get up on your feet, wipe the dust off your shoes, wipe the sweat off your brow, and remember you are too ligit to quit.

LESSON NO. 29

Keep your mouth shut, keep your
ears open, keep your eyes focused

I remember one day receiving a phone call from a friend. At that time I was still suffering the effects of what had been a very public failure. My friend said to me, 'Pat, where are you?' I was actually all by myself in the middle of a pity party, so I said to him, 'I'm having a party.' 'What kind of party?' he asked. 'A pity party,' I said, 'and I'm the only guest'. To which he replied, 'I want you to know that you were my friend before you were famous, you were my friend when you were famous, and now that everything has hit the wall, you are my friend now more than ever.'

I want to tell you that those words brought life to me more than you can imagine. Always remember, our words need to be chosen wisely. My friend knew to keep to the rule: keep your mouth shut, keep your ears open, and keep your eyes focussed. He kept his ears open to my heartfelt cries, he kept his eyes focused on our friendship, and he knew when to speak and when to shut up.

The good Lord gave us two ears and one mouth - we should take the hint. All of us sometimes want to shoot off at the mouth, especially in times of frustration. We want to blame others: our partner, our friends, and our business associates, but when we do that we only make ourselves smaller. During my time of challenge I opened my mouth way too much. I said things I never meant – too much said is too much heard and then it's too late. You can't take back words that are said. Sometimes the best words are not spoken.

In the heat of the moment, it is not the time to speak. It is a time to be silent. When everything inside you wants to explode you will say words that can't be taken back. Learn to keep your mouth shut and keep your ears open. People will say things that may hurt you, but you need to listen not just to their words but to their heart. One of the great lessons of life that we all need to learn is this: don't react to people's words. Instead, we must try to understand their pain.

During times of great challenge we often say things we do not mean, but people will judge us on those words. It is easier to respond to harsh words than relate to a person's pain. It is important to keep your ears open to what they are not saying. Don't just listen to what they are saying, look at their eyes: if they are

59

in a struggle, see their pain. Look at your partner's pain, your children's pain. Maybe it is not anger you are hearing, maybe it is fear. So often words are said and they sound like they have come from an angry heart, but maybe it is coming from a fearful heart.

There is a proverb that says, 'Out of the abundance of the heart, the mouth speaks.' Another proverb declares, 'The tongue has the power of life and death, and those who love it will eat its fruit.'

CHALLENGE

Your words will bring life or death. Choose life. Speak words of life to people. And as they build their lives, they'll help build yours.

LESSON NO. 30

A season is always seasonal; the tide always turns

I have come to realise that a season is always seasonal and that the tide always turns. Let me give you a few examples. Gloria Estefan was a gifted singer. Then tragedy struck and left her almost cripple. Nelson Mandela was a promising lawyer when he was imprisoned by a suppressive South African regime. During his imprisonment, the seasons moved on; the political climate changed. He walked out of that jail to find freedom to express his vision for a new South Africa. Michael Jordan was labelled a basketball failure in his youth: he didn't make the college basketball team.

Life sometimes ushers in Winter seasons during which we experience frighteningly cold periods, where our days are dark and lonely. Sometimes Autumn (or Fall) blows our way, and we feel that parts of our lives drop away like leaves from a tree and nothing seems to grow. But always there is Springtime, when everything we do blossoms, when projects suddenly begin to progress, when love is in the air and life couldn't be more beautiful. Then Summer rolls in like the surf, and our lives regain some fun and we take a break from all our toil.

The amazing thing is that no season lasts forever. But the good news, as one of my friends put it, is that we can extend the seasons. You can't control the seasons, but we can extend the enjoyment of a season. Whatever season you're in right now, whatever situation you find yourself in, understand that your season will pass. As that famous quote goes, "And this too shall pass."

You might be in a Summer season right now, harvesting great rewards and enjoying success. But take note that it is seasonal, and begin to store up for the Winter. Don't waste it all in the Summer. When Winter enters your world, you will be prepared because you've got a reserve tank in your car. Most people don't prepare for the unexpected. And sometimes the unexpected happens.

If you are in a season of Winter, where everything seems dark and dreary, make sure you look forward to the Springtime and Summer. If you want to get out of a difficult situation, give yourself time to think, time to strategise.

A wise friend told me once, 'If you're going through a dark tunnel, stay in the train.' Don't jump out of the train when it's in the tunnel. Wait until it stops. Wait until you get some light in the tunnel. And remember: there is always a light at the end of the tunnel.

Generally, farmers plant in the Winter and reap in the Summer or Spring when everything is blooming. The universal principle here is that you have to give up something to gain something. Something has to die before it lives. The seed has to die before it produces any kind of fruit. A cloud has to burst before it will produce rain. And they are all seasons: death comes first before life.

We all face seasons in life. Learn to understand that they are just seasons. As mentioned earlier in this chapter, Nelson Mandela's tide turned. He went from lawyer to prison mate to President. Gloria Estefan went from pop star to almost cripple to megastar. Michael Jordan went from failing to make the basketball team, to being the champion of the Chicago Bulls, to lousy baseball player, to great baseball player. These were their seasons.

Life responds to champions. Champions never quit striving for their goals and their dreams. Eventually, if you hang in there long enough through the seasons of hard times and challenges, you will discover that you will get opportunities to become successful and to overcome.

In his book *You Can Make a Difference*, Steadman Graham describes a photograph of a battered old rowing boat stuck on a sandbar in the ocean: "It was a pretty sad looking figure, this boat with its oars sticking up in the air, stuck on the sandbar. But the caption on the photograph was full of encouragement and hope. It read: 'The Tide Always Turns.'"

CHALLENGE

Right now you need to decide what season you are in. Then you've got to realise that time is your best friend, because every season passes. What is it that you can do now to prepare for the coming season? If you are in a season of Summer or Springtime, what can you do now to prepare for the Winter season? Should you be investing in the future? Should you be saving? Should you be making new contacts? Or perhaps you are in a Winter season. What can you do to prepare for a Summer season, for a season of fruitfulness, prosperity and success? Whatever season you are in right now, prepare for the next season.

LESSON NO. 31

What you've got ain't much, but it is all you need

We ought to be thankful for what we have, rather than peering around and wondering why we can't have what he's got or what she's got. While you are complaining about what you don't have, you can't appreciate what you do have. Sometimes we think, 'Why can't I have that person's wealth?' Maybe you need to be thankful for what you have and what you can do with what you have. Often we don't see the challenges, investments, decisions and sacrifices others have made on their road to success. We should not desire someone else's harvest when we haven't dirtied our own hands to sow the seeds that got them there. Be thankful for what you've got.

There is a tale told about a wealthy man's son who expected to receive a sports car for his graduation. Instead, his dad called him into his study, told him that he loved him and handed him a box. When the son opened the box he found a leather Bible with his name inscribed on the inside. Angrily he said, 'With all the money you've got you give me a lousy Bible!' He stormed out and never spoke to his father again. Years later the son received a call to say that his dad had died and left him everything. Going through his father's belongings, the son found that old Bible still in its box. Tearfully he noticed that his dad had underlined a verse of Scripture. It said, 'If you being evil know how to give good gifts to your children, how much more should your father give to them that ask.' As the son read the words, a car key fell out of the Bible. On the key was a tag with the dealer's name printed on it. The key belonged to the sports car he had wanted years earlier. On the tag, beside his graduation date, were the words 'Paid in full. Love, Dad'.

Sometimes we are like this young man. We complain about what we don't have and don't realise the treasure that is within our grasp. If we could only explore what we already have been given!

CHALLENGE

Today, be thankful for your family. Be thankful for the country you live in. Be thankful for the food you have. Be thankful for the freedom you have. Be thankful that every day you can live in safety and security. Be thankful that you have air to breathe, even though it may be a little smoggy. Be thankful for the little things, because they are a key that will open up incredible doors.

LESSON NO. 32

Your beliefs impact your life

Your core beliefs form the core of your life. Almost 95% of our actions we do unconsciously, and most of them are based on a belief system. Some have said that 85% of our belief system is in place by the time we are 18 years of age, and most of that is given to us from other people. Can you imagine, if your belief system is wrong, what kind of life you are going to live! We need to adjust our belief system to where we want to go and what we want to achieve in life.

Parents should also take note of this principle. In *Venus & Serena, My Seven Years as Hitting Coach for the Williams Sisters*, the former hitting coach of tennis players, Venus and Serena Williams, Dave Rineberg, writes that the sisters' father, Richard Williams, instilled a powerful belief in his daughters' minds that they would one day become tennis champions. "When they were 4 and 5 years old, Richard had that dream, and he kept them focused on it," Rineburg said.

Tiger Woods' father made sure his son grew up with a vision of who he wanted to become and how to go about achieving it. He groomed Tiger's mind and his body to be come one of the greatest golf players in history.

Everybody has beliefs. Believing is not just about religious doctrine. What do you believe about life? What do you believe about the way life turns out? Some people believe life just happens. Other people believe they are in the fate of some unknown force that uses us as pawns and we are just actors in this drama called life. You know, our lives are based on our beliefs. If our beliefs are wrong, our behaviour will be erroneous. Do you believe you need to constantly perform to get approval? If you do, you are going to be one very tired and frustrated person. Do you believe your success is based on luck or other people's acceptance or rejection of you? If you do, you will become a huge people pleaser.

In 1553, Admiral Richard Hawkins recorded that during his career on the high seas 10,000 men under his command had died of scurvy. He also noted that oranges and lemons (Vitamin C) prevented it. His observation went unheeded for over 200 years, during which time thousands of sailors lost their lives needlessly. In 1753, the British Naval Surgeon James Lind published a book saying that scurvy could be eliminated with lemon juice. He even cited case histories to prove it.

Instead of being honoured, he was ridiculed by the Lords of the Admiralty and by leading physicians of the day. In fact his advice was ignored for another 40 years. Not until a year after Lind's death in 1794 was a naval squadron supplied with orange juice on a voyage. On that voyage which lasted 23 weeks there was not one case of scurvy. Even so, another 10 years passed and thousands more died before regulations were put in place requiring sailors to drink a daily ration of lemon juice. With that enactment scurvy disappeared from the British Navy.

What a lesson in what we believe! People believed wrongly and others suffered. Your unbelief affects not only yourself, it also affects others. Beliefs affect everything about you. Your beliefs impact your day, your week, your years, your life.

CHALLENGE

Change your thinking, believe the best, and believe at all times. Here is a list of things to believe in.

- Believe that life is good.

- Believe that hardships will pass.

- Believe that you should not wait for your ship to come in, but that you should swim out to it.

- Believe that dreams come true.

- Believe that we have got to change so that we can really change.

LESSON NO. 33

Discover yourself to discover success

The greatest discovery you will make is discovering yourself. Who are you? I am not asking, 'What do you do?' or 'What is your function?' I am asking, 'Who are you? Who is (insert your name here)? What are your strengths? What are your weaknesses? What is your temperament? What are your gifts and your abilities? What makes you unique?'

We all have needs, desires and wants. Yet how can these ever be met unless we know what they are? All of us have an 'inner man'. That 'inner man' makes us who we really are. It thinks, it feels, it responds, it reacts, it learns, it has a will, it takes pleasure in certain things and displeasure in others.

It's a discovery of who you really are in life that will help you become what you want to be. So many people confuse their lives into a 'human doing' instead of a 'human being'. I am enjoying the wonder of discovering my wife and children: who they are and what they are. Yet I can only help them become what they desire to be by first understanding who I am and what I am in their world. Once you discover who you really are, you discover what relationships are important to you.

Can I encourage you not to be afraid to try to understand yourself more. It is one of the greatest discoveries you are ever going to make. How do you do it? Spend some time alone. Being alone doesn't mean you have to be lonely. It's simply 'alone time'. Read books on temperaments to find out what your temperament is. Ask some of your friends how they view you and what they see in you. Make a list of your strengths and weaknesses.

Lastly, develop an acceptance of yourself, because you can only truly appreciate others when there really is a true acceptance of yourself. Often we project rejection of others because we reject ourselves. On the one hand we want to be successful, wealthy, prosperous and happy, but on the other hand there is a feeling that we don't deserve it, we are not worthy of it, we can never make it. When you learn to discover who you really are, you will then begin to replace divisional thinking in your brain.

All of us at some point in our life fight with our own self. We want to do something and we don't. We don't want to do something and we do. One of the great mistakes in life is to measure ourselves by what we have accomplished, rather than what should have been accomplished by someone with our ability. You know, all of us have a lot more going for us than we ever imagine and if we learn to understand ourselves better I'm sure our lives would accomplish so much more. I used to believe that understanding other people's needs was my primary goal in life. But I found out that you can only understand others as much as you understand yourself.

Learn to understand yourself. What triggers you? What makes you tick? What makes you feel sad or rejected? What makes you feel like a winner? What causes you to have outbursts of anger? What causes you to keep restraint? Understanding yourself is the first and foremost key to life. Understanding yourself is the key to better relationships in business and at home. How on earth can you understand another person if you don't understand the one you live with - you! Somehow, we think it is humble to ignore our own needs. This is far from the truth.

All of us have basic human needs - a child in Rwanda has the same need for love and food as a child in Australia. Sadly, of course, the African child's needs are less likely to be met.

CHALLENGE

Maybe there are things in your life that you are starved of. It could be affection, a dream, a will to become, a sense of purpose. You have got to recognise areas in your life that you may be starving. If there is a need in your life that is going unmet, you have to address it now so that you can start growing. Discover yourself, and you will discover success!

LESSON NO. 34

What you feed grows, what you starve dies

When I was a child at school I had a teacher who enjoyed trying to scare the life out of me by sneaking up behind me and screaming at the top of her voice. I would be daydreaming and she would scream, 'Mesiti, pay attention!'

When I first started going out with friends my little Italian mother would yell out to me, 'Pasqualie, watch out when you cross the road, make sure you pay attention, cause if you get hit by a truck don't you come home crying to me.'

It is amazing how things happen in life that could be avoided if only we paid attention. The great lesson of life is what you feed or pay attention to grows, and what you starve dies. Some years ago I built a brand new home and decided to plant the gardens with beautiful flowers and trees. A green thumb was never one of my strengths, but I thought I would have a go. One year later, during a conversation with some friends, I mentioned how the plants were not growing well and that I thought the soil was not as good as the soil at our home where I grew up. One of my friends said in his deep South African accent, 'So the plants are not growing, Pat, is that correct? Have you tried watering them?' I suddenly realised I had wanted the plants to grow, I wanted beautiful blooms, but I didn't want to give them the attention they needed.

Too often we give too much attention to what is least important and too little attention to what is most important. Some people pay lots of attention to their physical body yet give no attention to their internal emotional and spiritual well-being. Other people spend a lot of time developing the inside – intellect, emotions, spirit - and don't care about the outside – fitness and appearance. Both matter.

Today there is so much trying to attract our attention: TV ads, music, meetings, catalogues, phone calls... But we must be the kind of people who pay attention to the things that help us build our lives successfully. You see, you can't ignore things and hope they will get better. You can't ignore your business and expect it to grow. You can't ignore your health and expect to stay healthy. You can't ignore things and expect them to stay the same or to get better. Instead, they will deteriorate. Consider your home - if you were to go away for two or three years and leave if totally untouched, on your return would the house and property be in a worse condition? Why? Because you neglected it.

What I pay attention to will progress; what I neglect will regress. Some people try to find faults rather than remedies. If all you seek are faults, that is all you will find. But if you look for remedies, guess what, you will find remedies.

I need to pay attention to my gifts and strengthen what I already have. What I pay attention to becomes my priority. Priorities don't happen by chance, they happen by choice. You can tell what your priorities are by what you spend your time on, where your thoughts are, and the projects you are most passionate about.

The thing that I pay attention to will give me reward. If you neglect your investments, they will not reward you, causing you a lot of financial harm. But if you focus and work on them, they will deliver rewards. Understand that many of the things that happen to us occur not because of fate or bad luck, but because we did not pay attention.

A little while ago, a good friend of mine was told that he had prostate cancer. It is a terrible disease. From what I understand, most prostate cancers should not happen if we would just pay attention to the symptoms and have them detected early.

CHALLENGE

Focus on those things that are important to you. What aspects of your life are being neglected and starved? Make sure you pay attention to the things around you so you don't suffer from neglect and regress. Negligence requires no effort, attention and focus require great effort.

LESSON NO. 35

The greatest remedy for anger is delay

Why would I address anger in a motivational book? The simple answer is everybody gets angry. Every day we hear people say, 'That person made me angry', 'That person made me mad', 'My wife/ husband made me angry', 'My boss makes me angry'. The truth is, anger is a choice.

I have learned that if you are angry and lash out, you generally don't achieve what you want. Anger is a natural part of life and it cannot be ignored. It must be managed. Amazingly, anger motivated Lee Iacocca to save Chrysler. He managed his anger in a positive way. You can be so angry about a situation that you will actually do something to fix it in a very positive way. You can prepare for action when you are angry. But never forget that you can do both great things and awful things when you are angry.

We all face anger, so how do we handle it? First, let me tell you how not to handle anger. Don't be aggressive. If we handle our anger using aggression we actually hurt people. If you kick the lawn mower or the washing machine, it doesn't make one bit of difference to those machines. Instead, you end up hurting yourself. That is a misuse of anger. Aggression does not alleviate pain. You can become hostile to the point where you hate someone or something.

But that is not the way to deal with anger. You see, we mainly get angry when something hurts our self-esteem, or stops us from moving forward, when something scares or threatens us. Some of us suppress our anger, others explode, and some punish themselves by talking negatively and looking down on themselves. People become easy prey to all kinds of neurotic and crazy behaviour when they get angry.

Use anger to control the pain that you are in. Anger and pain blind you, so be aware when anger and pain are approaching. I heard someone once say, 'He who has a sharp tongue soon cuts his own throat'. Friend, watch your words when you are angry. If you and I speak when we are angry we will make the best speech we will live to regret. Anger makes your mouth work faster than your mind and then you wonder what you have done. It is almost a moment of momentary madness, so learn to control your passion or it will control you.

71

CHALLENGE

The greatest remedy for anger is delay. Realise you are in the middle of pain, hurt, frustration or fear. Sometimes you want to get even, but you have to use your head not your emotions. Take time to think: get in between the pain and the action you are about to take. Think about why you are angry. Ask yourself what outcome you want to achieve. How can you actually get what you want without hurting someone else or yourself?

LESSON NO. 36

One good action is greater than a million good intentions

Have you ever met people who are always going to do something, they are about to do something, they were going to do something, but never actually did? People do not respect intentions, they respect action.

Many years ago I had the opportunity to be the executive director of a residential drug rehabilitation centre. It was in debt. It was in a mess. Nobody wanted to touch it, and I was full of good intentions and great feelings for these poor disadvantaged young people. But it wasn't until I actually got involved, took hold of the reigns, and turned that situation of debt around that I actually felt a sense of achievement. All the good intentions in the world, all the good feelings of emotion and feelings of compassion, didn't amount to anything until I got involved. That resulted in many young lives being changed.

Isn't it amazing how people judge themselves by their intentions, yet they judge others by their actions! They believe that if they *intended* to do something then it is actually done. We have to learn to be people of positive action, not professional procrastinators. Glean inspiration from this statement:

> *Did* is a word of achievement, *won't* is a word of retreat,
> *might* is a word of bereavement, *can't* is a word of
> defeat, *ought* is a word of duty, *try* is a word each hour,
> *will* is a word of beauty, *can* is a word of power.

Life is about action. Progress in life always involves risks and action. Former Chrysler Chairman, Lee Iacocca, says actions should not be confused with haste. How true that is. People run around so busy and so frantic yet they make very little progress because they are not people of decisive action. All of us need to understand that action produces results.

CHALLENGE

What is it right now that you are procrastinating about? Ask yourself if it is because you are afraid, because you don't know the outcome, or because you are not coping well. Develop an action plan that will take you to the level of living you want to achieve.

LESSON NO. 37

Earned love is an oxymoron

There are a lot of oxymorons around - phrases in which one word appears to contradict the next. For example, 'sanitary landfill', 'military intelligence', 'council worker'. I believe 'earned love' is an oxymoron too. You don't earn love, you give love irrespective of whether the beloved deserves to be loved. True love loves even the unworthy.

US psychiatrist, Dr Karl Menninger, said, 'Love is a basic need of human nature, for without it, life is disrupted emotionally, mentally, spiritually and physically.' We all need to be loved. As a matter of fact, it is the greatest need of all humanity. Alfred Lord Tennyson said that it is better to have loved and lost than never to have loved at all.

Isn't it amazing that in a game of tennis love means nothing, zero; but in life love is everything. Love is seeking to make another person happy. I used to say to myself, 'I just want someone to love me,' and then I realised that is the philosophy of an empty person. But to truly love you must seek to love someone. You see, you can only love out of fullness, you cannot love out of emptiness. You love your children, your spouse, and yourself out of fullness.

The story is told of a young soldier in the Korean War who telephoned his mother to say, 'Mum, I'm coming home.' The parents were so happy that they said, 'Son, we can't wait for you get home, we haven't seen you in a long time.' The son said, 'But Mum, Dad, I want to do one thing, I want to bring a friend home'. 'Sure son,' they said, 'bring as many as you like.' He said, 'No Mum, you don't understand, this friend of mine has suffered a lot through a bomb blast. He lost his right eye.' 'Well bring him with you,' the parents told him. 'He can come and be with us for a while.' The son responded: 'But Mum, you don't understand, not only did he lose his right eye, but he lost his right arm and his right leg as well.' His mother said to him, 'Son, we are so happy that you are coming home that we want you to bring friends, but don't you realize that after a while this boy is going to be a burden on us financially? If you want him to stay with us for a long time, you have to understand the challenges it presents us. We are going to have to restructure our home. This is going to be a burden for all of us, son, so just come on home. But bring your friend, he can stay for a while, but we can't have him stay with us forever.'

The young soldier hung up the phone. A few weeks later the parents received a letter from the military saying that their son had fallen from a balcony in his apartment. To their horror, when they went to identify the body, they discovered that the boy who had lost the eye, the arm, and the leg was their own son. He had been testing his parents to find out if his love had to be earned.

You see, earned love is an oxymoron. We choose to give it, and we must give it unconditionally.

CHALLENGE

My friend, today understand that you are special. You are loved. And when you understand that, it is amazing how much love you can pour into other people's lives. Maybe one of the reasons why people can't give love is because they have never been given love. They don't have it, because no one has given them love. But once you receive it, it is easy to pour it out to others. So receive someone's love today, and then give some of that love to someone else.

LESSON NO. 38

Your principles should be set in concrete, but not your methods

Change is the only constant in life. As a motivational speaker, my life has been all about helping people. You see, I learned that the principle is 'Help People'. Now, my method is normally to speak publicly, but I discovered other methods to help people. One of my gifts is the ability to raise finance for charities. Another one is to coach people, one-on-one, which I use in a corporate setting. I didn't have to be on a stage all the time to be helping people. The principle is to help people, but the method changed to helping charities raise money and coaching a small circle of people.

It is amazing how people can stick to one method of doing things. Some towns still ring the church bell because that's the way people used to announce church hundreds of years ago. Now they ring the church bells and everybody thinks it is a wedding. The congregation has never stopped to ask if this method is working or if there is a better way.

As great as Henry Ford was, he had poor people skills. When people wanting to buy his Model T Fords started asking him for a different colour car, he would answer, 'You can have any colour you want as long as it is black'. That's when his business started to decline. He believed that the Model T ended the need for any other car.

In the movie *Five Easy Pieces*, Jack Nicholson goes into a restaurant and asks for a side order of toast and when he is told it is not on the menu he comes up with a solution. He orders chicken salad on toast. Then he instructs the waitress saying, 'No mayonnaise, just butter and hold the chicken salad.'

CHALLENGE

If what you are doing is not working, you can either look for somebody to blame or you can look for a solution. You can find comfort that others are in the same boat and have a pity party. Or you can rationalise things and say, 'That's the way life is!' Or you can be willing to change. If something is not working, don't be afraid to change the method. Change is the only constant in life.

LESSON NO. 39

The greatest mistake you can make
is to be afraid of making a mistake

Larry Anderson, the former pitcher for the San Diego Padres, likes to say, 'If first you don't succeed, failure may be your thing'. While you can laugh at this statement, many of us fear failure and so cling to whatever we feel comfortable with, even if it does not work. We are afraid to invest, to take a risk. We are afraid that we will make a mistake. This is the sort of attitude that says, 'Don't look you might see, don't listen you might hear, don't think you might learn, don't make a decision you might be wrong, don't walk you might stumble, don't run you might fall, don't live you might die, don't change you might grow'.

In the 1940s, 80% of all watches sold were made in Switzerland. In the 1950s, a digital watch was presented to Swiss watchmakers and they rejected it because they already had the best watches in the world and the best watchmakers. The man who developed it subsequently sold his idea to Seiko and the rest, of course, is history. In 1940, Swiss watch companies employed 80,000 people; today they employ 18,000 people. In 1940, they made 80% of all watches; today they barely make 20%. This is what happens when individuals and organisations choose to die rather than change or become too afraid that they will make a mistake.

Author John Killinger said, 'Failure is the greatest opportunity I have to know who I really am'. I would add, 'Failure is the greatest opportunity to know what you might become'. You see, when it comes to mistakes, we overestimate the outcome and underestimate the process of learning. Every dream that has been fulfilled occurred because someone dared to make a mistake and did not get stuck in the failure. If you are not failing, you are probably not moving forward.

CHALLENGE

Don't live a life afraid of making mistakes. Mistakes are something we all make, but they are not all that we are. So go ahead, try it anyway!

LESSON NO. 40

'It is easy to be brave from a safe distance' - Aesop

Isn't it amazing how many people can give you advice on something they have never experienced? It is like the spectator who shouts to the sportsman what he ought to do and yet he has never been on the playing field. Bravery isn't about being loud or aggressive from the sidelines, it is showing resolve and strength in the forward line.

Poet Edgar A Guest puts it like this:

> Bravery is not a brilliant dash, a daring deed in a
> moment's flash,
> It isn't an instantaneous thing born of despair and a
> sudden spring,
> But something deep in the soul of man that is working
> always to serve some plan.

Bravery means you continue to live life even when you have no will to do so. Bravery does not mean that everything turns out okay. It is about having backbone and courage to act decisively even when you are scared half to death. DS Jordan said, 'Act brave. The world steps aside for the man who acts like he knows where he is going.'

There is something inside human beings that causes them to be brave in spite of adversity, in spite of hostility, in spite of the odds. I remember a discussion with a friend of mine who said true bravery is like a kite. A contrary wind raises it higher and higher.

You see, bravery is about falling but not yielding. Bravery is not giving in to what wants to drag you down and put you out. It is that quality in a champion that gets him up one more time when everyone thinks he is out for the count. It is about getting up and not giving in. Bravery is that quality of mind that makes us forget how afraid we really are, but we go on anyway.

To the brave and the true, nothing is difficult. You would be surprised how often bravery and sheer nerve succeeds. I have learned never to consult anyone who is a coward or anyone who has not faced adversity in life or business.

The simple prayer of theologian Reinhold Niebuhr sums up the spirit of bravery:

> God, grant me the serenity to accept the things that I
> cannot change,
> Courage to change the things I can,
> And the wisdom to know the difference.

CHALLENGE

Like a kite that rises higher in a strong and contrary wind, right now there may be contrary winds blowing against your life. The winds may be blowing against your marriage, or your finances, or your business. Now is not the time to run, now is the time to be brave. And allow the challenging winds lift you higher.

LESSON NO. 41

He who lives without control is exposed to ruin

One of the greatest gifts we can have is self-control. As a self-confessed control freak, I often try to control others and circumstances. But a fact of life is that people cannot be controlled and we really cannot control circumstance. You can't control the wind, but you can use it to your advantage. You can't control the weather, but you can control the atmosphere in your mind.

Why worry about things you can't control? Instead keep yourself busy controlling the things that depend on you. You cannot control the length of your days, but you can control the depth of your life. You cannot control the contour of your face, but you can control its expressions. Some of us lose control of our temper. Remember, the emptier the pot, the quicker the boil. We need to learn to control our thoughts; they may break into words and deeds we later regret. How true it is that 'a man's conquest of himself dwarfs the ascent of Everest'. He who lives without control is exposed to grievous ruin. So watch your temper.

Some people let their finances and their credit card debt get out of control. Some refuse to control their fantasy life or their pride. It may be a career that jeopardises your family. Learn to bring your life under control sooner rather than later.

If we spent more time in thinking of possible consequences, I'm sure we would bring our lives a little bit more under control. Sometimes when life spins out of control, we don't know how to bring it back, which causes more spinning out of control, and more frantic behaviour. Sometimes an out of control thought or action creates a situation in which other things spin out of control and it causes a rippling effect.

CHALLENGE

How do you bring your life under control? Think first, act later. Before you lose your temper, before you say a negative word, before you do the deed, think: what will the repercussion be?

LESSON NO. 42

There has never been a successful story half written

Michelangelo lay flat on his back for seven years to paint the Sistine Chapel. Charles Goodyear was obsessed with making a rubber that was unaffected by temperature extremes. Years of unsuccessful experiments caused him bitter disappointment, imprisonment for debt, family difficulties and ridicule from friends. He persevered and in February 1839 Goodyear discovered that adding sulphur to rubber achieved his purpose.

In 1905, the University of Bern rejected a doctoral dissertation saying it was irrelevant and fanciful. Albert Einstein was disappointed, but he wasn't defeated. Frank Woolworths laboured to save his first fifty dollars and then saw three of his first five chain stores fail. Many of life's failures are people who did not realise how close they were to success when they gave up.

Disappointment demands perseverance if we are to overcome. Disappointment comes to us all, but we need to get the 'dis' out of our disappointment and realise that we have an 'appointment' with success. To persevere in the midst of disappointment or being flat on your back is about choice. Perseverance is a decision of the will followed by a resilience in your soul.

You have to understand that in life we have to finish our course, we can't quit half way. They don't give medals for running half a race. We can't lose hope because hope is not passively waiting, it is an eager anticipation of what is to happen. In the meantime, while we are waiting, we do what is necessary to achieve what we need to achieve. You can be a failure at academics but be an incredible hero to millions of people. In school, Mohammed Ali came 376th out of 391 students, but he became one of the greatest champions in history—because he persevered. He suffered ridicule, shame, degradation and imprisonment for a little while, but now lives the rest of his life as a champion. Michael Jordan said, 'I failed over and over again in my life, that's why I have succeeded.'

Where you get advice from is very important. Can you imagine what your life would have been like if you had given up walking after the first baby steps, after the first toilet training mishap? Can you imagine if Pavarotti quit singing after his first music lesson, if Edison quit experimenting after 999 failures, or if Colonel Sanders quit after his first rejection? What if Winston Churchill had quit in the face of opposition from his fellow parliamentarians?

Understand that it is perseverance that gets results. There has never been a successful story half written, no successful song half sung. It is always too soon to quit. Thomas Carlyle spoke of 'permanence, perseverance and persistence in spite of all obstacles, discouragements and impossibilities. It is this that in all things distinguish the strong soul from the weak.'

CHALLENGE

It is imperative during the tough times to surround yourself with right choices and right voices. It is important *who* you listen to and *what* you listen to. It is important to read good books and listen to good tapes that will build up your spirit.

LESSON NO. 43

Your strength is in your struggle
and your power is in your pain

You've probably heard the saying "no pain, no gain". Growth always causes pain. Do you realise that your muscles will only grow as they tear? When you exercise your muscles, especially those you don't normally use, you will most likely feel sore in those muscles a day or two later. That's because, in using those muscles, you have actually torn them. The tearing will cause you some pain, but your muscles will end up with a greater capacity for strength. The next time you see a power lifter lifting heavy weights, just imagine the years of pain he had to go through to be able to lift that weight.

This principle also applies to our character. People with real strength of character are those who have overcome many hardships. The situations we struggle with and overcome can give us strength over time.

We all know people who seem to have everything going well for them and everything they do has a silver lining. But often we don't know how they reached that stage of success. Success is never instant, it is built over time. Nelson Mandela is a great example of someone who grew in stature as a result of many years of hardship. He went through an incredible struggle, yet out of that struggle grew strength, and he went on to become a great leader. His power came out of his pain.

A little old lady called Mother Teresa influenced a lot of powerful people to help her relieve suffering in India. Where did she get that power? It came from years of struggling to help the poor. Her power came out of her pain.

A few years ago Michael Jordan played in the NBA finals even though he was injured. During that game, he actually grabbed his own personal best records. You see, champions learn to play in pain. Endurance cyclist Lance Armstrong to date has won five Tour de Frances. But his successes are even more incredible when you realise his cycling days – let alone his life – could have ended when he was diagnosed with testicular cancer. He beat that cancer, got back in the saddle, and rode on to win more Tour de Frances. Today he is revered because people know his strength is in his struggle and his power is in his pain.

We often look at people who are successful and we think, "Well they haven't really been through much pain." Unfortunately, we tend to look at the instant poll or the snapshot of their lives at that point in time. We notice their nice cars, their great achievements, and their comfortable homes, but we don't see the pain that actually got them there.

You are most likely struggling with real issues right now. But guess what! Your current struggles are going to strengthen you. Your strength is in your struggle and your power is in your pain. In fact, your current struggles are going to give you credibility when you overcome them and begin to share your story with others. If there had been no struggle, there would be no story. If there had been no pain, there would be no victory.

When two opposing football teams face each other, there is a struggle for an hour or two. At the final whistle, the players stop and walk off the field in pain. But when does victory become sweetest? Victory is sweetest when the struggle has been fierce. An easy win is rarely sweet. When one football team annihilates the opposition, few people declare, 'Oh what a brilliant display, what a game!'

The same principle applies to relationships and to businesses. Relationships that don't go through struggles never get strengthened. Businesses that don't go through struggles never get strengthened. A life that doesn't go through struggles never gets strengthened.

M. Scott Peck says, 'It is only because of problems that we grow mentally, and spiritually.' Through the pain of confronting and resolving problems we learn. My great friend Ray Andrews said, 'All is not lost, but all is recoverable - find the positive'.

CHALLENGE

Look for the positives. No matter how painful a situation, understand that something positive can come out of it. Where does *your* strength and power come from? It comes from your pain. So what is it that is causing you pain right now? Remember, your struggles are going to strengthen you.

LESSON NO. 44

Don't lose your confidence - it is your
means of a great reward

Nothing steals your confidence more than ridicule. During a period of difficulty in my life I was being publicly humiliated on national television and in national newspapers. I wanted to hide in shame, but that's exactly what I would not do. My confidence was shattered. I felt I had been violated. In spite of it all, I still believed that something good would come out of the mess. Even though I did not have confidence necessarily in myself, I had confidence that things would turn out okay if I just learned to live one more day, to believe for one more moment. I said to myself, 'Pat, you've hit rock bottom, but the only way to look is up.'

You see, your attitude towards your failure or your disappointment determines your attitude after it. More than anything else, it is important to believe you have a purpose in life. Have confidence in that. You may think you have missed the mark, but as Dave Anderson says, 'Failure is the hallmark of success'. Failure can be the starting point of a new venture. When a baby learns to walk, it has to fall down a lot to learn the new skill. When a pole-vaulter finally misses in competition, it shows how far he has come. That failure becomes a starting point for his next effort proving that failure is not final. Failure is the hallmark of the success you worked for.

CHALLENGE

Confidence is contagious and so is a lack of it. It affects and spreads through every area of our life and every sphere of influence. Remember: if you lack confidence, so will those around you. Why do we lose confidence? Something may happen to us unexpectedly. Maybe we feel we have failed or we think others are better or more able than we are. Understand that your confidence is your confidence, not theirs. You are the hero in your story, the dream maker in your world. When you develop your confidence, others around you will develop theirs. So don't lose your confidence, it will bring you great reward.

LESSON NO. 45

First we make a habit, then the habit makes us

All of us need to develop good habits. Most of us have learned some bad ones. One of my negative habits is biting my nails. As much as I find it irritating, on occasions I still do it. But habits can be broken. That's what this book is all about—the daily things that we can do to reshape our lives. You see, habits make us or they break us.

Larry Bird, the basketball superstar, was filming a commercial when he was asked to miss one of his famous jump shots without changing his shooting form. His shooting form was not like that of someone who goes out and plays a basketball game in their driveway and shoots differently every time they shoot. Larry Bird's form was a finely tuned rhythm that his fans had seen consistently throughout his career. He was a shooting machine. The producer of the commercial waited patiently for Larry to miss a shot without changing his style or rhythm. He shot nine times before missing. He had created a habit and being asked to miss or change his habit was difficult.

We need to develop good healthy habits - eating habits, dress habits, speaking habits. I remember as a teenager I could not string together four words without two of them being swear words. Now my life is different because I have developed different habits. Some people want to change their habits and try once or twice and hope this will work. Psychologists tell us it takes 21 days to develop a habit and more than likely it will take more than 21 days to break it.

When you decide to implement a new behaviour it takes time for it to become a pattern. When you change your address, sometimes out of habit you still find yourself driving to where you used to live. When you get a new phone number, sometimes you still dial the old number by mistake. You have to catch yourself, stop, process, and replace the old habit with a new one. It feels awkward, but after a while you get the rhythm and you begin to form a different habit.

A change of habit can qualify us for a promotion. It can open the door for a new opportunity. It can increase our position and prosperity. It can add years to our life. It can help us develop good social habits, dress habits, giving habits, reading habits, exercise habits. These all become part of our lives that will teach us how to live a more productive life. Remember, old habits hinder new life.

CHALLENGE

What habit can you begin to break today? What new habit can you develop over the next 21 days? Think of it, then write it down. Make a decision that today will be the beginning of the rest of your life.

LESSON NO. 46

A dream won't make you something you're not, but it will make you everything you are

Many people have dreams hoping their dreams will make them something that they are not. Now, you can become better at what you are, you can increase your influence, and you can achieve more, but your dreams won't make you what you are not. Dreams can improve your life, but they can't help you become someone else. And in the process of trying to be someone else, not only do you fail, but you actually lose sight of your real dreams.

A dream won't make you something you're not, but it will make you everything you are. The book 'Soar with Your Strengths' by Donald Clifton and Paula Nelson opens with a parable. In the parable a duck, a fish, an eagle, an owl, a squirrel and a rabbit decide to become well-rounded animals. They put together a curriculum designed to teach them to run, swim, climb trees, jump and fly. By the end of the parable all the animals have tried to do something they were not created and equipped to do. Together they concluded that the best approach to life would be to have schools and businesses where people are allowed to concentrate on the things they do well. Rabbits would do nothing but run, squirrels would just climb trees, the fish would swim, the birds would fly. The point is that a dream can't always take you where you want to go, but it can always take you where you couldn't go without it.

Millions of talented musicians have dreamed of being signed up by a record company and having a number one hit, but only a few ever realise that dream. Most, however, find fulfilment in playing music. A dream will always benefit the dreamer. Even if the dream does not come true, you are always better off because you at least had a dream. The bonus is when a dream does come true.

Dreams are like faith in pictures or, as Barbara Cages describes it, a journey:

'The path to a dream is paved with sacrifices and
lined with determination. And though it has many
stumbling blocks along the way and may go in more than
one direction, it is marked with faith, it is travelled by
belief and courage, persistence and hard work.

It is conquered with a willingness to face challenges and take
chances to fail and try again and again. Along the way
you may have to confront doubt, setbacks and unfairness.
But when the path comes to an end you will find there is
no greater joy than making your dream come true.'

CHALLENGE

I want to encourage you to have a dream, your own dream. Get a vision of your
future. And then decide to enjoy your journey.

LESSON NO. 47

Everyone ends up somewhere in life.
You could end up somewhere on purpose

You and I should never live life in a hit-and-miss fashion. All of us should have a vision for life. If you don't, somebody else will. Vision is a powerful thing. Forrest Gump asked his mother, 'What's my destiny, Momma?' It was a question about vision, about what the future holds.

Without vision you will come to the end of your life and wonder about the things you could have done and should have done. Vision gives significance to mundane details. It is the difference between filling bags of dirt and piling them up in a wall to save a town against flooding. Filling bags is not glamorous, but saving a city from flood is worthwhile.

You see, vision involves emotion. There is no such thing as emotionless vision. Even the most lifeless routine can feel good when attached to a vision. The clearer the vision, the stronger the emotion.

Vision motivates us. If you were piling up dirt to save your town from flooding you would not be looking at your watch. You would not be sitting there bored. You would be focused on the vision. Filling those bags becomes a matter of life and death. You show me a person without motivation and I will show you someone with no vision.

Vision sets direction. People without a clear vision are easily distracted; they drift from one activity to another, one relationship to another. Instead, set your course, set your direction and pursue your vision.

Vision begins with a concern. When we have a vision we are consumed by what is and what could be. Perhaps your vision is to build a better financial base for your family, to feed the poor, to free a people from a tyrannical regime. All vision begins with a concern and that means all of us are candidates for vision.

Not all vision requires immediate action. Many people get a vision for something and think they automatically qualify to begin to fulfil it. We have to grow to fulfil our vision. For example, a little girl might have a dream of being a bride, and she will run into her mother's cupboard, take the wedding dress out, and put it on. For her, the vision is wonderful and clear: she will one day be a bride. But right now the dress doesn't fit. Like the little girl, we have to grow until we fit the vision and the vision fits us.

Unfortunately, time has proven that people who win the lotto or who inherit vast sums of money soon lose it. Why? For them, success came too quickly and easily. They didn't grow over time to earn their wealth. It came to them easily and suddenly, and that's a recipe for disaster. We've got to learn to grow to fit the vision of our lives.

Vision carries with it a moral element and a conviction that says something can be done and something should be done. It catapults you out of passive concern to urgency and action.

CHALLENGE

Our hearts must be moved with concern before we will ever begin to implement our vision. So let me ask you: What concerns you? What moves you? What breaks your heart? What makes you angry? What makes you want to rise above and stand tall?

My friend, answer these questions and you will find the cause that best suits you. Then build a vision around that cause. Because all vision requires someone to champion the cause. What is the cause that you can champion? What causes you to want to make a difference?

LESSON NO. 48

Where you stand determines what you see

One of the biggest lessons I have learned is that where you stand determines what you see. Life is about perspective.

A story is told of a brilliant musician who wanted to get to the top of the charts. After he finally made it, he reflected on his achievement and said, "When I got to the top I looked out over the horizon and found that there was nothing there." How sad! His perspective had once been that releasing chart-topping albums would bring fulfilment... it's what he had wanted, it was his dream. But when he got there, he was so disenchanted with his life that even all the trappings of success faded away into insignificance. It wasn't that he didn't achieve his dreams, but that his perspective had shifted.

Where you stand determines what you see. I heard a story about a shoe salesman who travels to Africa and discovers that nobody is wearing shoes. He becomes disillusioned and makes plans to return home immediately because nobody in Africa wears shoes. But another shoe salesman travels to Africa and on finding that nobody is wearing shoes declares, "What a market!" It's all about perspective.

Our perspective affects the way we respond to challenges. When we argue with others, we believe we are right and the other person is wrong. But when we consider the argument from the other person's perspective, and we see the challenges they are facing, the environment that has moulded their perspective, we discover that they are often right because they are viewing the argument from their perspective.

Perspective means that we put our own spin on things. That's because life impacts us all in so many different ways. And the way we respond to those challenges forms imprints in our minds called perspective. Next time you are in the middle of an argument, stop and look at it from the other person's perspective... and you may find they are also right.

Let me illustrate. When you stand on top of a mountain peak, the direction you face determines your perspective. Where you stand determines what you see. If you're facing north, you get a northern perspective. If you're facing south, you get a southern perspective. It's the same mountain, but you get many different perspectives.

Isn't it amazing how two people can be involved in an identical business, and yet one may succeed while the other one may fail! When it's all analysed and scrutinized, the underlying difference is their perspective.

I know two brothers who had totally different perspectives of their father. One of the brothers saw their father as a generous man, and yet the other brother saw his father as a complete tightwad who didn't do enough for him, even though the father had bought them both a car and a house. What was the difference? The one man was viewed in two very different lights.

It's amazing what perspective can do. You see it played out in the news media, in politics, and even in the courts. If you turn on the TV and see someone who's just been convicted of a terrible crime, you're often presented with two opposing perspectives all in the one news story: on the one hand you've got people representing the victims, crying out for justice, and on the other hand you see people displaying compassion, asking us to 'show them a bit more mercy'. What makes them differ? It's their perspective which is often developed over time by their own experiences. Are the opposing groups emotionally involved? Are any of them relatives of either the criminal or the victims? Their level of involvement and experience shapes their view of the situation.

I have faced many difficult circumstances over the past few years and, like you, I have a choice. I can either look back with regret and allow my life to spiral further downward, or I can choose to break out of the spiral and learn from my mistakes, failures, let-downs, and disappointments. Fortunately, I have chosen to move on and build something greater for the future. My perspective has made it easier for me to take this road.

We all go through similar challenges in life. We may be trying to achieve physical goals such as losing weight, or trying to start a business on a tight budget, or facing a difficult phase in a relationship. What's more important than the size of the challenge is our response to it. As I've often said, 'It's not what is taken from you that counts, but what you sow with what's left.'

CHALLENGE

How do you view life's challenges? What perspective do you have? What side of the mountain are you standing on? It's not too late to change your perspective. You can choose today to set your sights on a different view. Perhaps you need to climb a little higher up your mountain to enjoy a more colourful sunrise. Perhaps you need to step out from the shadows to choose your options under a brighter light. You see, your perspective is now up to you. Choose wisely.

LESSON NO. 49

You will not change until the pain of staying where you are becomes greater than the pain of change

Change doesn't occur by chance. It occurs by choice. And that choice is often triggered by something.

Over the years I have worked with many young men who were in the process of recovering from personal battles with addictions. Many times I watched parents who tried unsuccessfully to bribe their sons, to coerce their sons, to plead with their sons to break their addictive habits. The only people I ever met who had won their battle with addictive habits were those who had hit rock bottom. Their lives became so painful for them that they had to change.

To become successful, you must determine to beat complacency. Wishful thinking will not make you successful. You won't change, you won't become successful, until you're sick and tired of being sick and tired. Pain is a great motivator. Pain will cause you to get up and do something. Pain will get you back in the saddle.

How many people do you know who are relying on a lotto win to improve their lives? They want the house, the car, the overseas holiday, but it never happens. Then suddenly when the creditor is at the door, the house is about to be confiscated, the car is about to be repossessed, some pain hits them and they begin to do something about improving their lives.

One of my friends became an incredibly successful businessman after he was fired from his job. He didn't like his job, but it had been his security. When he was fired, the pain and humiliation caused him to choose between two options. One option he faced was to give up, thrown in the towel, and quit striving for a better life. His second option was to start his own business. He chose the second option, and today he's a multi-millionaire. The pain of getting fired and hitting rock bottom caused him to break through complacency to become the businessman he was destined to be.

It's the same in our relationships. You may be going through a very painful relationship right now. What are you going to do about it? You can either stay in that zone of pain, or you can want to change. Eventually, the pain may become so unbearable that you decide to do something about it.

You may have a habit, and that habit may not be detrimental to your health, but it may annoy your wife. Eventually you may get to a point where you decide, 'I can't handle the nagging any more, I've got to change!'

Some habits are detrimental to your health. One of my friends had a terrible problem with his weight. It wasn't until he had a massive heart attack that he decided to change his diet. He didn't change his diet because of the weight problem, he changed his diet when he had the heart attack.

CHALLENGE

Some of you may look at your life and say, 'I wish I had a better income' or 'I wish I had a better business' or 'I wish I could have a nice car'. Don't wait until it is too late to change. If the pain is already so intense, use that pain now to make a change, to break through into a better life, to start a new business, to apply for a new job, to invest time in your wife or husband, to wake up earlier each day to enjoy the sunrise.

LESSON NO. 50

Most people wait too long to get help

Failure and success are determined by two common elements: timing and advice. Most people who have succeeded received advice at the right time, from the right people, and acted on it. Most people who fail either received advice too late or received advice from the wrong people or decided not to act on correct advice. Failure to get the right help from the right people early can be costly.

A few years ago one of my close friends was diagnosed with prostate cancer. The tragedy wasn't so much that he had prostate cancer, but what he could have done to prevent the spread of prostate cancer. He went for help much too late. He continually postponed a visit to the specialist.

We are all a bit like my friend. We know what we need to do to become successful in our job, in our business, and in our relationships, but many of us fall prey to both timing and advice. Most people begin to face problems in marriage not long after their wedding day. Instead of dealing with issues early to prevent the problem from spreading, we tend to navigate around the problem over the years. This simply postpones the inevitable: at some point we must face a much larger problem because it has grown. Then we try to repair the broken relationship or business. One thing I have learned is that it's easier to manage something than to repair something.

It's smarter and easier to maintain a healthy lifestyle than to try to heal your body of cancer or heart problems. It's a lot easier to maintain a healthy attitude by conducting daily checkups of your attitude than it is to see your attitude slide and then try to rebuild it. I've seen so many people who appear to be positive, uplifting, and so fired up about life, but when tragedy hits, they get so negative because they didn't invest in their attitude on a regular basis.

It's the little foxes that spoil the vines. We tend to bypass the little problems and let them escalate into larger problems. Most addictive behaviour starts small. Most bankruptcies don't start as huge debts, they start as small problems that never get dealt with.

101

CHALLENGE

Become the kind of person who learns the power of timing and who looks for advice from the right people. Don't make the mistake of going for help at the right time and getting the wrong advice. Be sure to go to the right people for advice. If you are facing problems with your children, the last person you want to get counsel from is someone who has five kids and they're all in jail! Learn from someone with children who are happy and fulfilled.

What changes in your life are you putting off now that need to be implemented before it's too late?

LESSON NO. 51

You cannot move true north while your eyes are on negative south

Our minds are an incredible force. We gravitate towards the most dominant images in our minds. Many of us have heard the saying, 'It's not what happens *to* us that counts, but how we see them.' We don't see things as *they* are, we see things as we are.

What are the dominant images in your life and your business? Are they negative or are they positive? Are they images of success or images of failure? Why do I ask you this? Because your life will move towards the most dominant images that are in your mind. You see, your life cannot embrace what your mind doesn't believe. You cannot embrace success if you're constantly thinking failure.

Research has been conducted into how the mind can determine success. Experiments were performed on two groups of people who practised shooting basketballs into basketball hoops. One group simply visualised themselves throwing basketballs into hoops every day. The other group of people actually threw basketballs into hoops. The staggering result was that when they brought both groups together to throw balls into hoops, both groups came up with the same results.

You've often heard it said, 'What the mind can conceive, it can achieve.' Well the solution is to conceive them first. If you want a dream to come true, you've got to have it first. Your life will move in the direction of your dream because visualisation is a powerful force. Aristotle said that the soul doesn't think in words, it thinks in pictures. So whatever it is that you visualise, that is what you're going to move towards.

This also applies to the image we have of ourselves. Do you portray yourself in a negative or positive light? For example, parents who repeatedly tell their child, 'You're a naughty boy, you're a bad boy, you shouldn't be doing that!' could end up with a child possessing a negative image of himself. Those negative words are building an incorrect image in that child's mind. More than likely that boy is going to increasingly become a naughty boy. As one of my friends advised recently, 'If we tell a child who's just done something wrong, "You're a good boy, good boys don't do that", you're actually creating a positive image in that child's mind.'

103

I read recently that Jews comprise two percent of the world's population, yet they control 50 percent of its wealth. Another interesting fact is that one-third of all lawyers are of Jewish extraction. Now why is that? Because they are taught from the time they are children that poverty in a man's house is worse than 50 plagues. What's one of the dominant images in their psyche? That poverty is not a good thing.

In contrast, the Australian culture tends to demand a negative image of wealth. For instance, a typical Australian response to seeing an extremely successful person would be, 'He must be doing something illegal, he looks a bit shifty.' Our culture forms images in our psyche that dominate our lives and our attitudes to life.

How do we resist those negative images that invade our minds? We've got to renew our mind and renew the mental pictures we have of ourselves and of others. We are to create in our minds the kind of images that will enhance our lives, not hold us back... images that will lift us up, not draw us down. We've got to take charge of those images so that we can begin to enjoy lives of success.

We all make mistakes, but what sort of imprints of your mistakes do you form in your mind? Do you view them as once-off events or do you see them as a permanent condition? Do you say to yourself, 'I'm a mistake'? Or do you tell yourself, 'A mistake is something I did, not something I am?' What's the predominant image in your mind?

Do you have a predominant image of your financial situation? How you view money will determine your financial success. You might say, 'Gosh, I've only got $50 left!' Or do you do what my friend did and turn his only $50 into over $15 million! What was the image of money in my friend's head? That money, no matter what amount, is an opportunity to make more money.

CHALLENGE

Do you have a predominant image of your marriage, your business, your hobby? How do you view yourself in these areas? You are only going to progress towards true north when you get your eyes off south. You cannot go forward while looking in the rear vision mirror. Most of us need to break off the rear vision mirrors of our lives so we can make better progress.

LESSON NO. 52

Focus on what you have,
not on what you don't have.

The story is told of Rick Hoyt, a quadriplegic who could not speak. When he was born the doctors told his parents he would be a vegetable, but they determined to raise him like any other child. When he turned 10, Rick's life changed dramatically. Engineers at Tufts University created a device that enabled him to communicate via a computer. He painstakingly typed out his first words, 'Go Bruins!' That's when everyone discovered he was a sports fan.

After a long battle, Rick entered the public school system where he excelled. Two years later, when he found out about a five kilometre fund raising run to help a young athlete paralysed in an accident, he told his father he wanted to participate. His dad agreed to run and push his son in a modified wheel chair. They crossed the finishing line second to last, but that day Team Hoyt was born. They acquired a more sophisticated chair and the quadriplegic teenager and his out-of-shape dad began running together. In 1981 they ran their first Boston Marathon. Since then they have not missed one in 20 years. Rick has since earned his degree and works at Boston University helping design computer systems for people with disabilities. By March 2001 Team Hoyt had completed a total of 731 races, including 53 marathons and 135 triathlons.

CHALLENGE

Want to learn from this guy? He focused on what he had, not on what he didn't have. What about you? What do you have that is unique? What little do you have that you can turn into something? While we wait for the big break, the little opportunities that can open the door might pass us by. It's important that you focus on what you already have, and be grateful for it. Learn to use what you have now.

LESSON NO. 53

It is not what others believe about me that matters, it is what I believe about myself that matters

I have discovered that my life has often been given to people-pleasing. I have been concerned about other people's opinions much more than I should have been. However, it is not what other people think of me that is imperative, it is what I believe about myself that is important. God never begs anybody to believe in Him.

You too may be struggling to find your place in life. So let me tell you this story. Sparky did not have much going for him. In high school he flunked Latin, Algebra, English and Physics. He made the golf team, but promptly lost the only important match of the season. He then lost the consolation match. He was awkward socially, more shy than disliked. He never once asked a girl out on a date in secondary school.

One thing, however, was important to Sparky: drawing. He was proud of his artwork, even though nobody else appreciated it. He submitted cartoons to the editors of his college yearbook, but they were all rejected. Even so, he aspired to be an artist. After college, he sent samples of his work to the Walt Disney Studios. Again he was rejected, but he didn't quit. He decided to write his autobiography in cartoons. The popularity of his cartoon strip eventually led to countless books, television shows, and licensing opportunities. Sparky, you see, was actually Charles Schulz, creator of the Peanuts comic strip, possibly the most famous cartoon of all time. Like his main character Charlie Brown, Schulz at first seemed unable to succeed at many things, but he made the most of his talent and refused to quit and ended up at the top.

CHALLENGE

Now, my friend, why don't you go and do the same thing. Make the most of your talent, refuse to quit, and I'll see you at the top!

LESSON NO. 54

Begin again better than ever

Each time you plan, risk, fail, re-evaluate and adjust, you have the opportunity to begin again... only better than the last time.

Jonas Salk invented the vaccine that wiped out polio. But he conducted 200 experiments before he got the formula right! When he was asked the secret to his perseverance, he said: 'My family did not teach me in terms of failure, they taught me in terms of experience and what could be learned from it. I just made my 201st discovery, but I never would have made it out for the first 200 learning experiences.' John Maxwell, the brilliant author on leadership, points out that the difference between average people and achieving people is their perception of failure and their response to it. Most people fear failure because they are not properly prepared to handle it. Jeb Hubbard said, 'There is no failure, except in no longer trying; there is no defeat, expect from within; no really insurmountable barrier, save our own inherent weakness of purpose.'

There are two great truths in life: people die and people live. A few years back, as I faced one of my most difficult challenges in life, I felt like I wanted to die. Yet I knew I had every reason to live. Sometimes I reflected on what I would have changed, even for a day, if I had been give the opportunity again. The difficulties of the past felt almost insurmountable, yet I now feel I would not have changed any of them. That period of my life was probably the most shaping and character-building period of my life.

A universal truth is that people die, but a more powerful truth is that people live. And they live in the most remarkable ways, especially after setbacks, difficulties and struggles. Some of the challenges we face will never be understood, and neither should they. Our job is to understand ourselves in the midst of it all and become more successful and more productive.

A few years ago I ran five marathons back-to-back over five days and spoke 18 times at venues along the way. I remember someone said at the time, 'Man, it seems like you just fly up those hills when you run!' I know from experience that you don't fly up hills, you struggle slowly, painfully, and maybe, if you train hard enough, you get to the end of it and you survive.

CHALLENGE

Here are a few keys to turn your failure into success:

1. Get a new understanding of failure... a positive one.

2. Reduce your fears and get into action.

3. Change your response to failure by accepting responsibility.

4. Don't let failure get under your skin.

5. Kiss your past goodbye.

6. If you change, your world changes.

7. Get over yourself. Everybody else has.
   And start giving of yourself.

8. Find a benefit in every sad and bad experience.

9. Work on the weakness that weakens you.

10. Get up, get over it, and get going.

CONCLUSION

All of us are survivors and all of us are heroes. I want to close with a poem I wrote.

I am a Survivor

I have known the pain of loss and the joy of gain.
I felt the pain of an amputation called divorce
Then the exhilaration of a new found love.
I have suffered the agony of rejection
And yet bathed in the arms of acceptance.
I have suffered financial loss
But know the adventure of rebuilding wealth.
I have sensed the detachment of so-called buddies
But have felt the arms of acceptance from friends.
I have known the loss of reputation, the loss of dignity
The anguish of being frantic and confused
Yet I have seen the power of a clear horizon, a brand new vision.
I have known the feeling of shame enough to die
But known also the exhilaration of living because of the future.
I have faced my fear and now set my face towards a dream
For I am a survivor just like you
And we are not alone.

You see, all of us have a past. But more important to you is the fact that right now your future has no history. It's unwritten, unrecorded, not yet published. The great movie *Dead Poet's Society* made famous the words *carp diem*: seize the day! You have a choice to either let your future unfurl around you like a flag flapping in the wind... like letting the waves of change toss your boat this way and that... or you can grab the oars, set your direction to a spot on the horizon, and row into the wind, ignoring the muscle fatigue and blisters on your hands.

And as you row with all your strength, know this, that all great people have one thing in common: they all fail. But what sets them apart is their ability to learn from failure.

So grit your teeth and smile at the dawn because today you are in control of your future. You have a new direction, you've charted a new course, and no wind or rain or waves are going to stop you.

From now on you will continue to fail, but you will also taste much victory, smell sweet success, and touch triumph with both hands. From this day on, you are a winner, because you have chosen to learn. Congratulations!

If you've ever looked adversity in the eye and wondered how you'll ever rise above it to see another sunny day, this book reaches through the storm clouds to lift you higher than you've ever been before. Gifted motivational speaker and author, Pat Mesiti, will show you the view above your mountain and reveal simple steps to exploit your challenges to boost you higher above your circumstances. This book teaches you to soar!